Paul Henderson Scott's **A Twentieth Century Life** (Argyll, 2002) covered many diverse aspects – his safe and secure Portobello childhood and education at Edinburgh's Royal High School and University, his World War II years and his diplomatic career where he served worldwide.

Yet Paul Scott never lost touch with his native land and he returned to Scotland in 1980. Since then he has been an ambassador for Scots culture and letters and for Scottish independence. He has been Vice-President and arts spokesman for the SNP, President of the Saltire Society and of Scottish PEN and Rector of Dundee University.

The New Scotland is a twenty first century sequel in which the author writes on developments in the new century and gives pointers to the future.

Paul Henderson Scott lives in his native Edinburgh and has only recently given up skiing.

about **A Twentieth Century Life** . . .

"Scott has been a whirlwind of positive activity in the intellectual life of the nation . . . this is a belter of a book."
Alex Salmond in The Scotsman

"a delightful read. . . fluent and graceful"
Arnold Kemp

"A record of someone who has found himself at the hub, by accident, or by having the enterprise to find the hub, and set the wheel spinning. An absorbing read."
Ian Campbell in The University of Edinburgh Journal

"Written with elegance of style and constant flashes of wit. . . vivid cameos of life, painted swiftly, deftly and with complete frankness. . . That essential prop in life, a sense of the absurd, is constantly in evidence."
Alan Brooke Turner

"It is the best autobiography I have ever read."
Sir Neil MacCormick

"(a) splendid autobiographical volume"
The Scotsman

". . . may come to define a period of massive change . . . change which Scott influenced in a significant fashion"
The Herald

"a rare treat" **The Observer**

"evocative" **Sunday Herald**

The New Scotland

A 21st Century Sequel

Paul Henderson Scott

ARGYLL✠PUBLISHING

First published in 2008 by
Argyll Publishing
Glendaruel
Argyll PA22 3AE
Scotland
www.argyllpublishing.com

British Library Cataloguing-in-Publication Data.
A catalogue record for this book is available from
the British Library.

ISBN 978 1 906134 28 0

Cover Design: Based on an idea by Alasdair Gray,
portrait by Alasdair Gray

Printing: Athenaeum Press, Gateshead

for Laura

Contents

Introduction

For the last two or three years Harry Reid has been urging me to write a sequel to my autobiography, *A Twentieth Century Life*. Such suggestions from Harry have to be taken seriously. His judgement, in literary and other matters, is generally penetrating and shrewd. He proved this when he was the editor of *The Herald* and brought it to new levels of intellectual seriousness, a quality which is rare in newspapers and broadcasting these days.

Still, a sequel already to a book which I finished writing in 2000 and was published in 2002? In any case, I was fairly fully occupied with other projects. Of course, there have been great changes in the seven years or so since I wrote the autobiography. In its last paragraph I said that 'we stand on the brink of an exciting new age'. Now I suppose most people would say challenging or even frightening as well as exciting for it is remarkable how much the world has changed at about the turn of the century.

For about fifty years we had been living under the threat of a nuclear war between the Soviet Union and the West which could have destroyed civilised life on the entire planet. This seemed to end with the collapse of the Soviet Union. Optimists thought that the violent history of the world had at last ended and we were entering into a more rational and desirable time of international peace and collaboration. These notions were shattered with the attack on the Twin Towers in New York and the wild folly of the war on Iraq. The menace was now more subtle and unpredictable. Also the world was changing rapidly in other ways. Economic globalisation, rapid communication by computer, cheap travel by air and international organisations were eliminating space. At the same time cultural diversity was enhanced by the dissolution of the empires and the multi-national states. Climate change was a new and alarming threat.

Scotland itself is also in the middle of a revolution. The restoration of the Parliament in 1999 was a decisive first step, although the London government intended it to have the opposite effect. I said in the autobiography: 'the existence of a Parliament arouses expectations which cannot tolerate for long the trammels of reserved powers'. The end of fifty years of Labour Party domination of Scotland and the election of the formidable Alex Salmond as First Minister as a result of the election on 3rd May 2007 meant a complete change of mood in Scotland and a new spirit of optimism and confidence. We are well on the way to joining the ranks of the newly independent and previously submerged nations of Europe and to taking our proper place in the Age of Liberation.

So Harry Reid was right. Seven years is a short time, but in Scotland as elsewhere it was a time when old certainties were dissolving and new possibilities emerging. Much of the autobiography was concerned with steps towards these changes. It would not be complete without an account of this latest phase.

Paul Henderson Scott
Edinburgh, April 2008

1. A New Source:
The Files of the
Foreign and Commonwealth Office

My dear friend Anthea Perry, who served with me in the Havana Embassy, has been married for many years to George Findlayson. They now live in the south of France but usually come to visit George's family in North Berwick about the end of each year. On one of these visits Anthea told me about another former colleague in the diplomatic service who had used the Freedom of Information Act to get copies of his personal files from the Foreign and Commonwealth Office. I thought this would be interesting so I duly applied. Some time later a massive bundle of papers arrived. So massive that it was about a year before I found the time to tackle them.

I was staggered to discover how much time and energy the FCO spends in recording and analysing the qualities, or lack of them, and the performance of its staff. An embassy is usually quite a small and intimate community who work together and constantly exchange ideas both in the office and socially. You get to know one another fairly intimately. Your colleagues all have good degrees and have been selected by a long and careful process. They are likely to be highly intelligent and accustomed by the nature of their work to observing, analysing and describing the conduct of others, normally the members of the host government. The head of the post has to write a detailed annual report about his colleagues on a printed form of several pages. These in addition to comments by members of the FCO Personnel Department formed the bulk of the papers that now descended on me.

I seem to remember that the author of such reports is supposed to show them to the subject and at least to give an idea of their general drift. Perhaps I am wrong because I have no recollection of any of these and several of the points made in some of them surprise me. The only such document which I remember seeing before was the letter in which Personnel Department proposed me for appointment, perhaps to my first post abroad in the Embassy in Warsaw. I came across this accidentally in the file and one phrase I remember because it struck me as a memorable description which I hoped might be true: 'This officer is robust mentally and physically'.

The general tenor of all the reports, with one exception which I shall mention, was highly complimentary. In fact so much so that I hesitate to quote them because it looks like vanity. Still, perhaps I should because it is not often that one has access to frank and considered comments about oneself by intelligent people presumably making an effort to arrive at a fair judgement.

They begin with reports by members of the Selection Board at the notorious week-end house-party of intense investigation at Stoke D'Abernon in 1949. They could hardly have been more flattering.

> The manner of his performance is excellent in all respects. This officer is first-class. . . In quite a good group of candidates Scott was outstanding in the maturity of his manner. In the committee work he was the natural leader on account of his confident persuasiveness, his ability to argue his point clearly and concisely and his co-operative outlook which enabled him, to reconcile a number of differences of opinion.

The psychologist said: 'One could have no doubts about Scott's excellent representational qualities. . . He is a personable fellow and talks easily, clearly and fluently'.

I am pleased to see that several of the reports over the years

comment on my Scottishness. J.D.Murray (who was presumably
a Scot himself), the Head of South-East Asia Department, my
first department in the FCO, wrote on 31st March 1952:

> . . . displays most of the best qualities commonly
> attributed to Lowland Scots – which he is – especially
> dependability and sound common sense. On the social
> side he is not shy, but possibly a little stodgy and formal.
> He can be very good company once he has thrown off his
> initial reserve.

And he added a P.S. on 12th August 1952: 'has continued to do
excellent work. A sound and entirely dependable officer'.

In my second post abroad, La Paz in Bolivia, the Ambassador,
Sir John Garnett Lomax, also remarked on my Scottishness in
his report on 5th November 1956. It sounds as if he disapproved
of it:

> A Scot and probably a bit of a nationalist when he arrived,
> he seemed raw, uncouth and much on the defensive. He
> has improved immensely and he now gives his natural
> good qualities a chance. He has a naturally serious depth,
> but he knows how to be cheerful too.
> Sometimes have wished he was less obstinate in pressing
> his own views. He will make a first class Foreign Service
> officer. As a prospect, he is perhaps the best I have had. A
> studious person and an avid reader. Integrity beyond
> question.

R.E.Parsons, who was I think Head of Personnel Department
at the time, minuted on 15th December 1972: 'an independent-
minded Scot, kind-hearted, but obdurate and outspoken'.

I have the impression that what some of these reports call
Scottishness, others call dourness, social awkwardness and
stubbornness. Perhaps this reflects a difference in Scottish from
English social behaviour. I think that this distinction was more

marked in the Edinburgh in which I grew up before the War than it has since become. Since that time the BBC (which was founded in 1922) has exerted a strong influence in favour of English social behaviour and speech. In pre-war days it was common to hear expressions of astonishment and disapproval of English behaviour which was considered excessively demonstrative, flamboyant and insincere. It was the Scottish habit, possibly a consequence of our Presbyterian inheritance, to cultivate a somewhat formal reserve, except among close friends. We also believed in saying what we thought, not what we were expected to think.

The most striking example of what I think was an English misunderstanding of Scottish social attitudes is in a report by Sir Peter Wilkinson, Ambassador in Vienna:

> His energy and enthusiasm seem unlimited. His manners
> are uneasy and he lacks social charm (which he might
> despise). He is a cool customer and hard as nails. I should
> expect him to fight his way out of any personal tight
> corner, quite ruthlessly if need be.

I do not recognise myself in this description, but perhaps I appear so to a man used to English social manners. I seem to make quite a different impression to others. There is an undated Personnel Department minute which says:

> I like Mr Scott who is gentle, sensible and kindly. He
> would be out of place in any job requiring great drive or
> inspiration.

But Wilkinson's report is not typical. To display English generosity of spirit, this was the report of 18th September 1967 by Sir William Oliver, the British Commissioner General for Expo '67 in Montreal. I was his deputy:

> The British Pavillion has been an outstanding success at

Expo '67. . . It is no exaggeration to say that is in large measure due to his determination and energy far beyond the normal call of duty that our Pavillion has been the enormous success that it is.

With a minute staff his work has been quite phenomenal. Working long hours day and night far beyond the call of duty he has borne the burden and heat of the day and overcome difficulties that would have daunted many.

An excellent French speaker he quickly gained the confidence not only of the Expo authorities, but of the Municipality as well. His flair for constant but quiet publicity and his instinct with the press gained Britain an advantage which has never been lost.

But I promised to mention the most adverse of the reports. It is a slightly amusing episode. This was from Sir Peter Hayman who was High Commissioner in Ottawa when I was Head of Post in Montreal. The first of his reports about me was dated 23rd October 1972. It begins quite favourably:

Mr Scott is intelligent. He has a taste and flair for political work: he has imagination and energy. But I am afraid that he does not find vital fulfilment for his talents in Montreal. . . He is in robust health: he skis very well.

His final comment at the end is: 'All in all, I rather like him but he is undoubtedly one of the most 'awkward' people that I have ever met in my official career!'

The damning part of the report, which is eighteen pages long, is in a brief table which calls for an indication of overall performance by a tick in a box and is meant to be a summary of the whole thing. Hayman placed me between 4: 'Fair: performs duties moderately well and without serious shortcomings' and 5: 'Less than Adequate: Definite weaknesses make the officer not quite good enough to get by'.

Clearly this was bad enough to bring my career to an abrupt

end if it was taken seriously. Fortunately, an Inspector, Mervyn Brown, inspected Ottawa and Montreal shortly after Hayman's report. The head of Personnel Department, Richard Parsons, asked him to look into my performance and relations with Hayman. Brown's reply is the next document in the file. He says:

> I formed a favourable opinion of Mr Scott's good sense and judgement. He seemed to us to have a sound view of what his Post should be doing and of his own role in Montreal. Political reporting, which is important and which he does mostly himself, is well done. His office is in general well run and staff relations are very good.

He goes on to explain the reasons for Hayman's attitude:

> We understand that the High Commissioner has criticised Mr Scott for not meeting him at the airport when he visits Montreal and has insisted that in future both Mr and Mrs Scott should greet him and see him off. This would be a reasonable proposition if the high Commissioner made only a few visits to Montreal in a year. But during the month before our inspection Sir Peter Hayman visited Montreal or passed through no less than 5 times. A journey to and from the airport, including waiting time at the airport, can take up to 2 or 3 hours and it seems to me an improper use of a Grade 3 officer's time to expect him to act as a meeting and greeting officer.

This was in fact the reason behind all the fuss and Hayman's discontent with me. He was quite a likeable man with some good qualities, but he had a grossly exaggerated idea of his own importance. He expected not only elaborate deference at airports, but a reception like a Head of State when he arrived to stay at a hotel, the flag flying and the manager and his staff lined up to meet him on the pavement outside. I had to try to restrain him to avoid absurdity.

It happened that I had reason to visit London shortly after this report and as a matter of routine I called on Personnel Department. There is a long minute by Richard Parsons. At one point, he makes a familiar point about Scottishness: 'Sir Peter Hayman likes plenty of attention from his staff and Mr Scott is an independent-minded Scot!' He then goes on to say:

> In the circumstances I thought it right to speak reasonably
> frankly to Mr Scott who is an old friend. I told him that
> Sir P. Hayman seemed to feel a bit frustrated with him,
> and that there seemed to be differences between them
> both on policy and about method of working. I did not,
> however, disclose the full horror of Sir P. Hayman's report
> on him, both because the High Commissioner had clearly
> failed to tell him just how bad it was. Mr Scott reacted well
> to what I said. He said everyone knew Sir P. Hayman. He
> was an autocrat and liked everyone to fuss around him. It
> was just one of those things that the staff in Canada had to
> live with. Mr Scott said this with humour and without
> rancour, and I was impressed by the mature and almost
> affectionate way in which he spoke of his High
> Commissioner in the circumstances. Mr Scott said he did
> not think we should make too much of his differences with
> Sir P. Hayman who was mercurial and could fly into rages
> but be very nice afterwards. He commented that there was
> in fact a major policy difference between them.
> He himself wanted to cut out the independent post in
> Quebec, which would make his own post in Montreal
> much more worthwhile. This was opposed by Sir P.
> Hayman, but supported by the Inspectors. It was all very
> awkward.

This storm in a tea-cup ended quite amicably. There is a minute in the file by the Chief Clerk (a misleading title for the Under-Secretary in charge of the Administrative Departments and the final arbiter on personnel matters). He recalls a meeting with Hayman on 11th January 1974:

> P. Hayman went out of his way to speak well of Mr Scott in Montreal of whom he had previously been a rather devastating critic. . . He was an able man but could be extremely obstinate.

There is also a minute by the Chief Clerk, D.C.Tebbit, of 14th March 1973:

> I had a rather agreeable conversation with Mr Scott whose grasp of the Canadian scene appeared to me to be rather impressive.

Hayman himself mellowed in the end. His later report about me on 19th March 1974 concludes:

> My last report was not very favourable. But thanks to his own very real ability – assisted by one or two broad hints from Pers.Dept. and from me – he has done very well in the last 18 months. He remains obstinate to a fault, and we do not always see eye to eye but I respect his judgement. He at least goes through the motions of respecting mine!
> On a personal note, I should add that they could not have been kinder or more helpful over the forthcoming marriage of our daughter.
> Paul is a fine and courageous skier.

Finally, in defence of my reputation, quotations from two other reports. From Sir Anthony Rumbold in Vienna in 1969:

> A very satisfactory Chargé d'Affaires. . . behind his slightly dour appearance and manner, he conceals a lively intelligence and an engaging mind. . . solid as a rock and

I rely on his judgement. . . the British Community much admire him and he seems to have lots of Austrian friends.

From Sir Alan Campbell in Rome in 1977:

He is clearly a most intelligent man, indeed a very interesting one in many ways.

All of this would have been a useful source available when I was writing the autobiography. Now it is a digression and in the next chapter I turn to the new theme. ❏

2. The Parliament Reconvened

My autobiography ended just as two longstanding objectives had been achieved: the reconvening (to use Winnie Ewing's term) of the Scottish Parliament after nearly 300 years, and the decision by the Parliament itself to establish a National Theatre. I had desired both of these for most of my life and I have campaigned actively for both since I came back to Edinburgh in 1980. It is a common experience that the realisation of an aspiration often fails to meet your expectations. That might be said of both of these, but both are only beginning and have the potential eventually to do all that we might expect of them.

The formal opening of Parliament on 1st July 1999 was a day of evident delight and enthusiasm on the streets of Edinburgh. The ceremony itself, which I saw on television, admirably caught the mood of the time. Tom Fleming read a poem by Iain Crichton Smith in which he spoke of 'our three-tongued country'. Donald Dewar made a speech redolent of the spirit of the Scottish past. Sheena Wellington, a few yards away from the Queen and the Duke of Edinburgh, sang Robert Burns' celebration of Scottish egalitarianism:

> Ye see yon birkie ca'd a lord,
> Wha struts, an stares, an a' that?
> Tho hundreds worship at his word,
> He's but a cuif for a' that.
> For a' that, an a' that,
> His ribband star, and a' that,
> The man o independent mind,
> He looks and laughs at a' that.

If the Parliament and the enthusiasm of the people at large had continued in the same spirit, Scotland would have been transformed; but it has to be admitted that the Parliament failed to meet its early promise and the people were soon disillusioned. There were several reasons for this.

The major reason was the attitude of the Labour Party which formed the Government in coalition with the Liberal-Democrats. From Dewar's public speeches and from the few conversations I had with him, I think that he was genuine in his Scottish enthusiasm. When he introduced the Scotland Act in the Westminster Parliament he read out the opening sentence with obvious relish: 'There will be a Scottish Parliament,' and he added, 'I like that'.

But the Labour Party as a whole was not really at ease with the emancipation of Scotland. Over the years their policy had fluctuated. When the first group of Scottish Labour MPs were elected to Westminster in the early years of the twentieth century, they said that they would soon be back in a Scottish Parliament. Home Rule remained Labour policy until 1950 when it was dropped. It was revived in the 1970s as a response to the rise of the SNP, but many of their own MPs were unhappy with it. One of them proposed an amendment to the effect that approval in the Referendum of 1979 would require a positive vote of 40%, not of those voting, but of the electoral roll. This virtually impossible requirement amounted to deliberate sabotage. Many Labour branches in Scotland gave very little support to the campaign.

It was certainly different in the next referendum in 1997 when Donald Dewar campaigned happily with Alex Salmond. Perhaps this was because the Labour Party as a whole believed that George Robertson was right when he said that a Scottish Parliament would kill the SNP and Scottish Independence stone dead. How wrong he was.

In fact, I think that other, and disastrous, aspects of Labour policy show that their leadership were not at all sure about Robertson's theory. It was evident at the time, and Labour supporter and journalist Tom Brown confirmed it when he spoke at a debate in the Royal Society of Edinburgh on 9th March 2004, that Labour candidates were deliberately chosen as a group who would obediently follow official policy and have no ideas of their own. The result has been that the Labour members for the most part have been a very unimpressive bunch.

For the same sort of reason, a fear that the Scottish Parliament might adopt politics that would advance Scottish distinctiveness and self-confidence and therefore assist the SNP, Labour policies for the most part have been very unambitious. In spite of their hesitant, off and on, approach to the idea of a Scottish Parliament, Labour spokesmen frequently claim the entire credit for its successful creation in the end. In fact, the referendum campaign in 1997 depended very heavily on the support of Alex Salmond and the SNP. Before that, the issue had been kept alive by the Campaign for a Scottish Assembly (as it was originally called) leading to the compelling statement of the case in the Claim of Right of July 1988. As I was well aware, because I was one of them, most of the work behind this campaign was done by a small group of people of about my own age. The historian, Christopher Harvie, who is now an MSP, said in an article in *The Scotsman* on 31 January 2004:

> Titter ye not, MSPs. Without the likes of Robert Grieve, Paul Scott, Jim Ross and Kenyon Wright you would not exist.

He has repeated the point several times in the books which he has written since then.

What are the reasons for the hostility, or panic fear, of the Labour Party to the whole idea of Scottish independence? This applies more to the leadership than to their supporters in Scotland many of whom, according to opinion polls, are in favour of it.

I suppose that one of the underlying, if mistaken, causes is a conviction that the welfare state and the National Health Service are due to the Labour Party and that they alone can be trusted to maintain them. There might even be a fear, which Labour propagandists do their best to encourage, that an independent Scotland could not afford them. Then the bloc of forty-odd Scottish Labour MPs at Westminster have not only a comfortable and well-paid job for themselves but provide reliable support for a Labour Government. Labour has more than once been in power in Westminster only by virtue of these Scottish votes. Tony Blair, in spite of his large majority, depended several times on these same votes to pass measures affecting Education and the Health Service in England, although Westminster MPs have no responsibility for these matters in Scotland.

Few governments willingly give up territory that has been useful to them. When the Union was under discussion in 1706 Daniel Defoe, as an official propagandist in favour of it, in one of his pamphlets intended for an English audience wrote:

> Scotland was an inexhaustible source of men who would enable England to play a greater role in Europe than it had ever played before.

It has certainly done that and not only in Europe but in the Empire while it existed and in many wars, including Iraq.

In more recent times British Governments have been able to assume control over the income from the oil in Scottish waters which properly, under international law, belongs to Scotland. In January 2006 papers released under the Freedom of Information Act showed that studies by Treasury officials in 1970 had shown that the discovery of oil in Scottish waters could make Scotland a very rich country. One concluded that 'income per head in Scotland could be 25% or 30% higher than that prevailing in England during the 1980s given independence'. Both Labour and Conservative ministers deliberately concealed the facts and succeeded in diverting income from oil to the Treasury in London. Fortunately enough oil still remains for another thirty to forty years.

Scotland also provides a base on the Clyde for the submarines with nuclear weapons which no English constituency is likely to welcome. In the age of global warming, Scotland provides a potential source of water and of wind and tidal energy. In other words, Scotland is a useful asset to England. If it were a liability, as much of the popular press in England seems to believe, British Governments would not be so keen to hold on to it.

The deficiencies of the Labour/Lib.Dem. coalition were not the only reasons for the early disillusionment of much of the Scottish people with the restored Parliament. One was the building itself and in particular with the cost soaring out of control from an early estimate of £40 million to a final total of over £400 million. In fact, responsibility for this did not rest with the Scottish Parliament itself but with the British Government which took the vital decisions about the architect, design and site and construction contracts, responsible for the costs, before the Parliament was constituted. In fact, most of these were the personal decision of Donald Dewar as Secretary of State for Scotland. It is said in his defence that he was anxious to commit the Government to a prominent and expensive new building before it changed its mind about devolution.

Since Barcelona is famous, or notorious, for its idiosyncratic and eccentric architecture it was a brave decision to choose a Catalan architect, Enrico Miralles, and again Donald Dewar seems to have been the force behind the decision of the small selection committee which he appointed. At an early stage of the process I was invited as President of the Saltire Society to a small gathering to see an exhibition of the various designs which had been proposed. Both Dewar and Miralles were there and were evidently in close rapport. At that stage the proposals of Miralles were extremely vague. Shortly afterwards I attended a lecture which he gave in the Chambers Street Museum. At the end there was time for only a couple of questions. The first reflected the feelings of us all, I think, when the questioner began by saying that after listening carefully he had to admit that he had not been able to form any idea of the nature of the building, could the speaker at least say what material would be used. Miralles replied, 'Oh, I have no idea: it will gradually evolve.'

Most of us would probably consider that a building to house the first Scottish Parliament to meet for 300 years should have a building which looks Scottish and reflects our architectural traditions. In fact, not surprisingly, the new building would look more at home in Barcelona than in Scotland. I find the exterior incongruous and ugly. The only attractive part is Queensberry House, with its notorious associations, which has been finely restored or rather enhanced. The gloomy public reception area of the new building is more suitable to escape the heat of a Barcelona summer than to welcome visitors on a cool and dull Edinburgh day. In the chamber I think that the modern desks are over-elaborate and rather absurd. They conceal the members and give the impression that the place is empty. The rest of the building, and the committee rooms especially, are eccentric and fussy. Nothing is standard, but all is specially designed, expensive to install and to maintain. But I find that many of the people who work in the building like it, and it has been praised by the architectural press and won architectural awards.

Yet another cause of public discontent with the Parliament was the high salaries paid to the members and the newspaper reports that many of them seemed to be playing fast and loose with their generous allowances. Of course, it is worse at Westminster where the regulations are less strict. Shortly after the referendum over devolution in the North of England, Robin Cook the Foreign Secretary who had the decency to resign over Blair's decision to join in the invasion of Iraq, gave a speech in Edinburgh. One of the points he made was that the referendum had failed because of the current unpopularity of politicians.

I asked him if that was not, at least partly, because people had been given the impression that many parliamentarians were there just for the money. Would it not be better if they were paid only the minimum wage? The idea evidently took him by surprise, but after some hesitation he said that he thought they should be paid the rate for the job. That, of course, raises more questions than it answers.

Perhaps the strangest reason of all for the unpopularity of the Scottish Parliament during its first eight years was the virtually unanimous hostility of the press. Many newspapers missed no opportunity to criticise and deride it. In the past, *The Scotsman*, especially when my old friend Alastair Dunnett was editor, had campaigned vigorously for the restoration of the Parliament. When it was established, *The Scotsman* led the abuse. Indeed as long as the paper was under the direction of Andrew Neil on behalf of the owners, the Barclay brothers, it often seemed not only to be anti-Parliament, but anti-everything Scottish. Fortunately this is no longer true since it has been acquired by the Scottish company, Johnston Press.

But popular discontent with the Parliament in its first few years never reached the point, according to all the opinion polls, where many people regretted its existence. A majority consistently wanted it to have more powers and many people agreed with Tam Dalyell that its existence would lead irresistibly to independence.

In the early months of 2007, before the Scottish Election in May, Edinburgh University held a series of lectures and debates about the Union of 1707 in recognition of its three hundredth anniversary. All of them had large audiences of several hundred people. The last was in late April in the Assembly Hall of the Church of Scotland, where Parliament had met until its new building was ready.

The four speakers were two Professors, Harry Reid who is in favour of independence and Allan Massie whose position on the matter is complicated. During a discussion on BBC Newsnight Scotland about his book *The Thistle and the Rose*, Allan Massie was asked about this. He replied that his position was one of conflict between his reason and his emotions. It was not unlike the attitude of many people in the past to Jacobitism. In their minds they were convinced that there was no alternative to acceptance of the Hanoverians, but in their feelings they longed for the return of the Stewards. Intellectually, he was convinced by the case for Scottish independence, but in his emotions he was British.

In the assembly hall after the four speeches and the discussion by members of the audience, Magnus Linklater, began his final remarks by saying that it was clear that the Union, of which he was personally in favour, was no longer the flavour of the month. He was interrupted by Massie: 'No, it is now obvious that Tam Dalyell was right.'

Apart from watching television coverage of debates on television fairly regularly, my own experience of the Parliament has been with one of its potentially valuable innovations, the Cross Party groups. The idea is to provide a forum where MSPs can meet and exchange ideas with specialists or enthusiasts in particular subjects. This could be a very useful channel to inject proposals into the parliamentary machine. In my experience, so far at least, it has not really worked like that. It has been more of an opportunity for enthusiasts to let off steam which can then be safely ignored, a sort of safety valve. Usually the only MSP who attends is the one appointed to act as the convener. In the first session the only such Group to which I belonged was on the Scots Language. Irene McGugan, an SNP member from Dundee, ran it with efficiency and enthusiasm. A few of the many Labour Ministers of Culture, none of whom stayed very long in office, attended the occasional meeting. They listened with apparent attention and agreement but that was the last we heard of it. We were particularly hopeful for action by Lord Watson because he expressed agreement with rather more apparent understanding and enthusiasm than the others. Unfortunately he was imprisoned shortly afterwards because of his drunken attempt to set fire to the curtains of Prestonfield House.

The Group did however produce one result of potential significance. Colin Donati, Joy Hendry, James Robertson and myself were asked to produce a Statement of Principles which should apply to the Scots language and relate it to the Universal Declaration of Linguistic Rights, which was signed in Barcelona in 1996 (Autobiography, p.289). The Statement was published as a pamphlet in March 2003 and distributed fairly widely, but so far without any visible effect.

The other group to which I have belonged was on Scottish Writing and Publishing. It was started only after the 2004 elections with Chris Ballance of the Green Party as Convener. Its last meeting before the 2007 elections was on 24th January and, significantly enough, its agenda included a strong paper by James Robertson in which he said that the Scots language, 'a core element of Scottish culture. . . still suffers from an almost total neglect by government'. It ended by a demand in the first instance for the teaching of the language and literature throughout the educational system and in the longer term it should be given 'official status and recognition equivalent to that accorded to English and Gaelic'. Alan Riach spoke eloquently in favour. I suggested that the phrase 'longer term' could be used as an excuse for indefinite delay and we should demand immediate action.

Of course, it is highly satisfactory that Gaelic has been given recognition and support. It is an important part of Scottish tradition, the oldest surviving language with a long history of contribution to Scottish life, rich in song and poetry. Scots has a shorter history, but one of many centuries. It is spoken or understood by more people than Gaelic and it is one of the pleasures of Scottish life. Much of our best poetry, including of course that of Robert Burns, and many of our best plays are written in it. It is a rich and expressive language and many aspects of Scottish life, experience and attitudes become alive in it as they do in no other tongue: snell, dreich, smeddum, stravaig.

If our bairns are allowed to grow up speaking both Scots and English, which is quite possible because they have much vocabulary in common, they become bilingual quite naturally and without effort. This is a great advantage in life because bilingualism is a stimulus to intelligence and an encouragement to appreciate the subtleties and variations of vocabulary. It makes the acquisition of other languages much easier, especially as Scots has much common vocabulary also with German, Dutch and the Scandinavian languages.

Why then were the Labour/Liberal-Democrat administration, and perhaps also Scottish officialdom, so reluctant to give Scots its proper place in Scottish life? A consultation paper produced by the Cultural Policy Division of the Education Department of the Scottish Government in February 2007 said that 'Scots is not an endangered language'. Did they mean not a language or not under threat? I suspect the former. It then went on to say that 'the Scots language will be treated with respect and pride', which sounds like an excuse for doing no more.

I have the impression that officials tend to think that Scots, unlike Gaelic, is not a distinctive language because of its common origin and much vocabulary with English. But that is not unusual among languages. It can be said of Scottish and Irish Gaelic, or Swedish, Norwegian or Danish, or of Spanish and Catalan. You do not have to read, or listen to, much Scots without realising how distinctive it is. Then perhaps they have been brought up by their parents or schools to regard Scots merely as vulgar or wrong English, a deplorable slang – 'Dinnae say dinnae; speak proper'.

I think that this last point is one which applies to many members of the Labour Party, even to those who, I have experienced myself, are perfectly capable of speaking fluent Scots. They have been made ashamed of it. Then there is another more political point. It is harmless enough to support Gaelic because not enough people speak it to have dangerous political effects; but Scots could potentially be spoken by most people in Scotland. It might increase Scottish awareness and confidence. If they are encouraged to enjoy their own language, might that not encourage them to want to govern themselves?

Apart from these Cross Party groups, the Scottish Parliament has introduced another politically very useful facility. This is the Petitions Committee which enable members of the public to petition the Parliament to take action on an issue which concerns them. In 2000 George Reid (not the future presiding Officer but a member of the Saltire Society with the same name) raised the question of the correct shade of blue in the Saltire Flag. For years there has been embarrassing and absurd confusion with the Saltire, the oldest national flag in Europe, ranging from the dark blue, which is used in the Union flag, to various lighter shades. I have always thought that it should be a light sky blue which would reflect the legend of its origin at the battle of Athelstaneford in 832. When the Committee first discussed the matter the Convener proposed no action on the grounds that neither the Parliament nor the Lord Lyon King of Arms had the power to decide. Accordingly, with the help of the Presiding officer David Steel, I wrote, as President of the Saltire Society, to the Lord Lyon. The new holder of the office, Robin Blair, sent me a detailed and very helpful letter on 20th April 2001 in which he said that it would be appropriate for the Scottish Parliament to decide the matter.

Armed with this, I had a long correspondence with the Deputy First Minister, Jim Wallace, the leader of the Liberal-Democrats. He produced one reason after another why the Scottish Executive could take no action. I answered each of them in turn and made the obvious point that it was for the Parliament and not the Executive to decide. I sent copies to all MSPs. George Reid raised the matter again with the Petitions Committee in May 2002. The St Andrews Society and the Heraldry Society for Scotland joined in the pressure. Finally the Parliament reached the desirable decision that the colour should be a light blue, Pantone 300 in the international colour code. George Reid and I think general opinion had prevailed in the end.

This is only a small demonstration of the ability of the Parliament to respond to public pressure and change conditions in Scotland for the better. In spite of all the discontent with the performance of the Parliament in its first eight years and the drastic limitations in its powers and subordination to Westminster, its mere existence has transformed Scotland. It has reminded the Scots themselves and the rest of the world that Scotland still exists with its own needs, qualities, aspirations and the right to be heard. ❑

3. The National Theatre and Other Cultural Aspirations

As stated in the last chapter, the recovery of the Scottish Parliament was rapidly followed by the decision to establish a National Theatre. This was, encouragingly enough, one of the first important measures taken by the Parliament. As I mentioned at the end of the last chapter of the autobiography, the Parliamentary Committee, to which I gave evidence, made its recommendations in February 2000. Since, like many people, I had campaigned for both of these things for many years, I was naturally delighted.

The National Theatre which emerged, like the Parliament itself, was very different from the one which we had hoped to see. During all the discussions and reports which had followed the Advisory Committee on the Arts in Scotland (AdCAS) Conference in 1987, and even before that, there had been clear agreement about the most important function of a National Theatre. This was to rescue from oblivion the many excellent Scottish plays, mainly from the previous century, which had successful productions but had then disappeared because there was no company committed to the development of a Scottish repertoire. Of course, the National Theatre should also stage new plays and others from abroad, but the main purpose was to repair the neglect of the past. Every other national theatre in the world has a primary responsibility for its own national body of plays. As Joyce McMillan said in the *Charter for the Arts in Scotland* which she wrote for the Scottish Arts Council in 1993:

The case for a national theatre rests on the contention that it is absurd for Scotland, which has little indigenous tradition in ballet and opera, to support major national companies in these areas, while having no national theatre to protect and express our much richer inheritance of Scots drama and theatrical tradition. It is also pointed out that, although Scotland supports a rich network of theatre companies, none of them has a specific remit to perform and develop Scottish repertoire and languages.

That then was the major purpose. A second one was to have a company (to quote Joyce McMillan again). . .

whose remit it is to preserve, develop and promote the Scottish dramatic repertoire, to encourage Scottish writing for the stage, and to help actors and directors acquire and maintain the language and performance skills necessary for the most effective performance of drama in all forms of Scots and in Gaelic.

The campaigners had no doubt about these two purposes. There was possibly less certainty about the need for the National Theatre to have its own building and company of actors. My own view was both were necessary in the longer term. In the past there had been two companies which were embryonic national theatres, the Scottish National Players and the Scottish Theatre Company. Both had found that they were undermined by the lack of their own building to stage whatever they wanted to perform. A building also gives a sense of identity, solidity and continuity. At least a nucleus of actors is desirable to produce the benefits which flow from working together.

In the autobiography (p.284) I mentioned a meeting of the AdCAS working party on the campaign for a National Theatre in December 1988. One of the participants was Frank Dunlop who was then Director of the Edinburgh Festival. He spoke out very strongly against any idea of watering down our original proposals, that is to say against anything less than a company with its own theatre:

> It is tragic for Scotland that this sort of thing happened so often. We shall not achieve anything unless we aim high . . . Edinburgh had the capacity to become a world capital of intellect and art, but there were too many people in authority whose outlook was provincial and who were prepared to be dominated by London.

The Scottish Arts Council (SAC) responded to our campaign by the customary tactic to avoid a decision, the appointment of consultants to write a feasibility study. In the past the establishment of a National Theatre had been one of the major objectives of the SAC, but more recently it was obvious that they had changed their mind. As Magnus Linklater, then the Chairman of the SAC, was frank enough to say to me in August 1999: 'We already have enough trouble with the existing national companies without having another one round our necks.'

The Arts Council had briefed the Parliamentary Committee and it was therefore not surprising that in recommending the establishment of the National Theatre the Committee adopted the more cautious and cheaper option of no building and no company. But they did add that this was 'a starting point which, if successful, would allow the development of more advanced models.'

Following this recommendation in February 2000, the finance minister announced in September 2003 that the formation of the National Theatre would go ahead with an initial budget of £7.5 million over the next two years. In October 2003 applications were invited for the post of Chairman and members of the Board of Directors. I duly applied and had a letter from Donald Findlay on 15th June 2004 to say that he had been appointed to the chair and would I still be interested in becoming a board member. I agreed and had quite an interesting interview in the following month.

In March, Findlay wrote to say that they were 'unable to accommodate' me at present, but would I allow my name to remain on the file. This did not surprise me. Apart from being so closely identified with the alternative view of the nature of the structure that was needed, I was 83, which most people seem to feel is an automatic disqualification for almost any position. I was however pleased that my fellow campaigner, Donald Smith, the Director of the Netherbow Theatre (now the Scottish Storytelling Centre) was made a member of the Board.

The next step was the appointment by the Board in July 2004 of Vicky Featherstone as Director. Her previous post was as Director of an English touring company, Paines Plough, which was described as specialising in new writing. It had made a good reputation for itself and had appeared in the Traverse in Edinburgh. Apart from that, her only experience of Scotland had been between the ages of six weeks and seven years when her father had been employed by BP at Grangemouth. Her accent was described in the press as 'vaguely estuary'. In the hope that it might give her some idea of our expectations of the National Theatre, I sent Vicky Featherstone a number of my books of collected papers which included some about the project. I received no acknowledgement or reply.

On the other hand, when I sent copies of some of the relevant correspondence to Richard Findlay, he replied and invited me to a discussion. He asked about a point in a letter I had sent to the Secretary of State, Malcolm Rifkind, shortly after the AdCAS Conference about a National Theatre in 1987. I had said: 'We do not believe that an expensive new building is necessary.' He asked if that meant that we had thought of something like the present arrangement? In fact our proposal was that some existing building should be used, such as the Lyceum in Edinburgh. That would be very suitable. Every other National Theatre in the world has a building in the capital.

We were soon to discover that the absence of a theatre building and its own company of actors were not the only ways in which the National Theatre was to be quite different from the ideal for which so many people had campaigned for years.

Featherstone took up her appointment in November 2004 and in March 2005 she was due to give a talk about her plans in the Lyceum Theatre in Edinburgh, but she had been invited, apparently at short notice, to have lunch with the Queen. Her place was taken by John Tiffany who had been appointed to the National Theatre as director of new work. He is a Yorkshireman who was literary director of the Traverse from 1997 to 2001 and during the time Paines Plough had put on there a few of their productions. At the end of his talk he was asked when the new National Theatre would stage the *Thrie Estaitis*. Tiffany dismissed the question as an irrelevance. 'We do not feel a responsibility to revisit Scottish classics'.

At about the same time he had been reported as saying that Scotland was a country with no dramatic tradition. Featherstone seems to have much the same view. On 14th August 2005 *The Scotsman* reported a discussion between her and Annie Ryan, the author of *Dublin by Lamplight*, a play about the turbulent beginning of a National Theatre in Ireland. Featherstone was quoted as saying: 'I think there's a big heritage in Ireland that's a pressure on you, which I don't think that Scotland has in quite the same way.'

Of course, it is precisely because Scotland has a large body of great plays which we seldom have an opportunity to see that was one of the main impulses behind the demand for a National Theatre. David Greig in an essay on this subject in the *Sunday Herald* of 14th March 2004 said that we should not 'preserve old languages, old plays or old writers simply for the sake of cultural heritage' but 'to use the work of the past to speak to the present'. That is the point. It is important to be able to see these plays, partly because they illuminate the past, but also because they still have something pertinent to say to us.

The Association for Scottish Literary Studies (ASLS) publishes an annual volume of Scottish books of the past which are still important. The most recent three of such volumes are of plays, *Serving Twa Maisters: Five Classic Plays in Scots Translation* in 2005,

The Devil to Stage: Five Plays by James Bridie in 2006, and *Scottish People's Theatre: Plays by Glasgow Unity Writers* in 2007. This is a demonstration of the importance of our dramatic tradition. At the last meeting of the Council of the ASLS we decided that the subject of our annual conference in 2008 would be drama and we would invite Vicky Featherstone. It should be an interesting discussion.

During the 2006 Edinburgh Festival Featherstone gave a public lecture which I attended. In the question session, I asked her if she had seen the pamphlet, *The Scottish Stage*, which Donald Smith had edited for the National Theatre campaign in 1994. It contained a list of more than 200 plays which had been recommended for consideration by a National Theatre. She said that she was aware of this list and six people, including herself, were reading through the plays to consider them for possible production. Of course, many of our best plays are in Scots which may be difficult for the members of the National Theatre organisation who are not Scottish and have no appreciation of the language.

David Lindsay's *The Thrie Estaitis*, written in about 1552 is a special case, the origin and inspiration of the Scottish dramatic tradition. I quote Joyce McMillan again – she is after all one of our best and most experienced dramatic critics. She wrote in *The Scotsman* on 16th March 2007:

> Sir David Lindsay's great *Satyre Of The Thrie Estaitis* is the
> cornerstone of all Scottish theatre, a mighty satirical
> pageant of the human condition – and of the body politic–
> – that not only became a huge popular success in its day,
> but seems to re-emerge at every major turning point in
> Scotland's theatre history. It is our only surviving
> vernacular drama from the age when Scotland was a state
> in its own right, its tongue not only the language of the
> street and of popular comedy, but of law, religion, poetry,
> romance, philosophical argument and political power. The
> language of the play, therefore, has a range, a confidence,

an urbanity, and a rich comic sophistication that was soon
to become rare in Scots-language writing; and it's perhaps
small wonder that its key twentieth century revivals – by
the legendary Tyrone Guthrie at Edinburgh Assembly Hall
during the Edinburgh Festival of 1948, and again by the
Scottish Theatre Company in 1986 – have both had an
electrifying effect on Scottish audiences and artists,
alerting them to all the huge forgotten possibilities of the
national language and culture.

She is right about the 'electrifying effect' of the Tyrone
Guthrie production in the Edinburgh Festival of 1948. It is my
most powerful memory of all the great performances I have
seen in almost all of the sixty festivals. The excitement and
delight of the audience at this rediscovery of the Scottish past
was inescapable. The production was repeated in 1949. There
were others by Bill Bryden in 1973 and by Tom Fleming in
1985, which won an international prize in Warsaw in the
following year.

Since then there has been no other performance of *The Thrie
Estaitis* in the Edinburgh Festival, except once a modern
imitation of it. This is astonishing, not only because of its
outstanding popularity in the past, but because Brian McMaster,
who was Director of the Festival from 1992 to 2006, said in one
of his first press conferences that he would stage *The Thrie Estaitis*
every two years or so to give an element of continuity like
Everyman at Salzburg. I reminded him of this more or less every
year at the launch of the programme. He came close to a
production one year by the Glasgow Citizens Theatre, but it
failed to appear. As soon as the formation of the National
Theatre was announced McMaster said that he could leave a
production to them 'because it was bound to be one of their
first priorities.' He was right about that, but there is no sign
that the present National Theatre agrees.

Certainly the National Theatre has made a contribution to
Scottish life. In particular the play *Black Watch,* by Gregory Burke

and directed by John Tiffany, has been very successful and is touring to London and the United States; but so far there has been no sign of any attempt to demonstrate that Scotland has an important theatrical tradition which can add to our understanding of the present.

Still the same point applies to this as to the Parliament. The first step is to have the institution even if at first it is imperfect. Once the institution exists, it can change and develop. Donald Smith has told me that he is confident that the National Theatre will eventually evolve in the direction for which we all campaigned. I hope he is right.

•

Since it began in 1922 broadcasting has been the greatest threat to the survival of the distinctive values of Scottish civilisation. In his inaugural lecture as Professor of Scottish History in Edinburgh University in 1980 Geoffrey Barrow said that 'failure to create a Scottish organisation for public service broadcasting was the most serious cultural disaster which Scotland suffered in the twentieth century.'

From the introduction of radio and subsequently television the great majority of programmes which have reached virtually every house in Scotland have emanated from London. There have certainly been some good Scottish programmes from the BBC, Scottish Television and other broadcasters, but the overwhelming majority have been English. Their view of the world, contemporary affairs and history, their achievements, assumptions and attitudes have been the major force in this most influential means of communication. In a phrase used by Gus MacDonald, when he was Chairman of Scottish Television, we were threatened with the loss of 'the ability to create images of ourselves and to conduct arguments within our own society.' The Scottish audience have been made to feel insignificant and unimportant, as if we were the inhabitants of a country which had achieved nothing and where nothing of any importance had ever happened. It is not surprising if, as many people believe, the Scots have lost self-confidence and ambition.

The recovery of the Scottish Parliament should have given us an opportunity to improve matters, but this was frustrated by the inclusion of broadcasting in the long list of powers reserved to the Westminster Parliament. The Labour Government evidently believed that it would be dangerous to trust the Scots with such an important means of influencing attitudes and opinions.

Inevitably therefore the situation has not improved but has deteriorated. As Iain MacWhirter powerfully demonstrated in a column in *The Herald* on 23rd July 2007 the two most important producers of TV programmes in Scotland, Kirsty Wark's company, Wark Clements, and Muriel Gray's, Ideal World, have both been sold to a London based company because otherwise they could not get commissions from channels based in London. Network commissions from the BBC, ITV and Channels 4 and 5 have halved in the past three years from 6% of the UK total to about 3%, a loss of about £40 million a year. On a population basis the BBC should spend about 9% of its budget in Scotland, but it has been spending only 4%. Blair Jenkins, the former Head of News and Current Affairs in BBC Scotland, said in *The Herald* of 18th June 2007, that expenditure on current affairs in television in Scotland (that is by the BBC and STV) had declined between 2001 and 2006 by 45% and on news by 27%. He resigned in consequence and called for an all-party attempt to remove broadcasting from the list of reserved matters.

Iain MacWhirter's conclusion was that all of this amounts to:

> . . . creative clearances which pose the most fundamental challenge to Scottish society. If there is no medium which authentically reflects Scotland's culture and politics, how can we conduct a coherent national conversation? If we see ourselves through the distorted prism of a London media,

how do we know who we are? And how do we talk to the
world instead of just to ourselves?

The Saltire Society has been concerned about broadcasting
for many years. Since the Scotland Act was published in 1998 I
have argued that broadcasting should not be a reserved matter,
that BBC Scotland should become autonomous and that Ofcom
should be replaced in Scotland by a Scottish organisation. *The
Scotsman* and *The Herald* both reported these views in December
2006. The Saltire Council discussed the issue and the Chairman,
Ian Scott, launched a campaign. He organised a meeting in
February 2007 which led to a conference in Napier University
on 18th May at which Alastair Moffat and Alan Riach spoke
effectively. Since then the campaign has contiued.

There are many other objectives for which I have campaigned for years along with the Saltire Society, the Scots Language
Society and the Association for Scottish Literary Studies. They
include recognition and support for the Scots language (which
I discussed in Chapter 2 and which has been a particular victim
of the domination of broadcasting by London); Scottish history,
literature and languages in the schools; the encouragement of
our traditional music and dance.

Since UNESCO recognised Edinburgh as the first City of
Literature in 2003 I have been conducting a personal campaign
for the establishment of a comprehensive Writers' Museum in
Edinburgh, a National Museum of Scottish Literature. Apart
from all its other purposes, it is now a necessary part of
Edinburgh in its new UNESCO role. Imagine a visitor attracted
to Edinburgh because he has heard that it is a City of Literature.
He hears that there is a Writers' Museum in Lady Stair's Close.
He hurries to it, only to discover that it records only three writers,
although certainly major figures, Burns, Scott and Stevenson.
Imagine his reaction. World City and that's all they have!

Well, of course, we do have very much more, in several
languages and for centuries. We should make all of this evident,
not only to enlighten the visitor, but our own people. It would

be a valuable educational asset, and a place for literary meetings and discussions. It would provide visual evidence of the richness of the literary tradition of Edinburgh and Scotland, but also show that it was still vigorously alive with events about and with contemporary writers. The National Library and the Central, Signet and Advocates Libraries, the existing Writers' Museum and Makars' Court are all very close together in the centre of Edinburgh, close to the High Street. We should aim at the same area; the former Midlothian Council Chambers would be ideal.

In the last four years or so I have been enlisting support for this idea to all the various organisations concerned with literature. All are in favour of the proposal. Above all, Martyn Wade, the National Librarian in charge of the National Library of Scotland has told me that the idea accords very closely with his own developing ideas. This is vital because the resources of the National Library would be an essential source for the new Museum and it should be a national institution as an adjunct to the Library itself. It only now requires the new Scottish Government to give its approval.

There are many battles on the cultural front that have to be fought time and again. One of the most important is the contribution of music composed and plays written by Scots to the programme of the Edinburgh Festival. Usually the Director is appointed from outside Scotland, knowing little or nothing about the Scottish contribution to music or drama or anything else. Frank Dunlop and Brian McMaster both responded well, but in different ways, to the obvious need when it was demonstrated to them. So far the new man, Jonathan Mills, has not yet had time. I addressed my opening appeal to him in an article in *The Scotsman* on 12th May 2007. So far, he has not responded.

All of the objectives which I have discussed in this chapter are important because they are stimulants and expressions of Scottish culture which has contributed so much to Scotland and to the rest of the world. The fundamental reason why Scotland should be independent is because it is the home of this culture which can only flourish if we have control of our own affairs. In the words of The Claim of Right of 1988: 'The Union has always been, and remains, a threat to the survival of a distinctive culture in Scotland'. ❏

4. A Crowded Decade

I have never had any doubt that Edinburgh was the place which I most enjoyed, felt most at home and was where I wanted finally to settle down. Probably most people feel like this about their native place; but Edinburgh, it seems to me, has many positive advantages. Childhood memories and literary and historical associations are a factor, but other qualities are still more important. For one thing, parts of it are very beautiful. I often stand on the terrace of the New Club in Princes Street, look across the gardens to the Castle and the Old Town and feel that no other city can offer a comparable view. Another which gives me pleasure that never tires is from my own sitting-room in Drumsheugh Gardens to Inchkeith, a large expanse of the Firth of Forth and the hills of Fife beyond.

But even more important than the views is what goes on in this place. I have often remarked in my diary that living in Edinburgh is an opportunity for continuous education. There is a never ending series of lectures, debates, exhibitions, and so forth and most of them free to all comers. Once you are known to be interested in that sort of thing, you get a constant stream of invitations through the post. Then there are the theatres and concerts, for most of the year not so many as in a large city like London, but enough. There is the torrent of activity in August with the Festival, the Fringe and the Book Festival when the world comes to Edinburgh.

Then the people. There is a vast army of admirable human beings in all the organisations of which I am a member. The SNP, Saltire Society, Scots Language Society, Scottish PEN,

AdCAS, the ASLS, the National Trust for Scotland (especially those associated with the cruises on the *Black Prince*), the Sir Walter Scott and R.L. Stevenson Clubs, the New Club and the Scottish Arts Club.

In the autobiography there is a melancholy passage about friends who have died (pp.304-7). They included my closest ally, Bert Davis and I now have to add my oldest friend of all, Donald Cameron, who was in my class at the Royal High School. David Daiches too has gone and I recently had the sad task of writing an essay for a book about him, edited by an American, William Baker. This is appropriate because of David's work in American universities. He had a formidable knowledge of most of the great literatures of the world, but the one closest to his heart was the Scottish.

In reading again this passage in the autobiography I was struck by the number of poets among those whose friendship has mattered to me. I thought of it again recently when I was writing a review of David Robb's fine biography of Alexander Scott, *Auld Campaigner*. Perhaps there is something about poetry which makes poets friendly and agreeable companions. They have included Sorley MacLean, Iain Crichton Smith, Robert Garioch, Hamish Henderson, Jack Aitken and George Bruce. I met Hugh MacDiarmid and Sydney Goodsir Smith on several memorable occasions but these were brief encounters when I was on leave in Edinburgh. I had both friendly and argumentative encounters with Norman MacCaig. It is always a pleasure to meet Edwin Morgan, Stewart Conn or Alan Riach.

Although I usually confine myself to prose, I have written a verse or two now and again. At least one of these, *Reikie 2,000*, has been published. This was in a collection, *Edinburgh: An Intimate City,* edited by Bashabi Fraser and Elaine Greig in 2000. George Bruce and Stewart Conn both told me that they liked my poem. It ended on an optimistic note:

> But noo there is a glisk o hope.
> At last we hae oor Parliament back.

Reined in yet by Westminster,
But sune we'll ding thae traces doon.
Ower lang oor caws for equality and social justice
Hae fallen on deif and distant lugs.
Sune we shall bigg a new and fairer Scotland
Wi Reikie a real capital aince mair.

Another extract, but not, as far as I remember, of this last stanza appeared in an exhibition in the City Art Centre. Laura also had a poem in the same book, *Impression of Edinburgh,* and this had the distinction of being made part of a display in Edinburgh Airport to welcome visitors to Scotland. The poem ends:

Streets swept by northerly wind;
A multitude of fragrances
Fill the daily air.
From commanding hills
Gray gradients run precipitously downwards
And vanish in a glimpse of sea.
This unique city,
Which one cannot fail to love.

Of course, I also had friends among writers in prose. When I came back to Edinburgh in 1980 one of my oldest friends, Suzanne Sinclair, was living in Great Stuart Street. She introduced me to George Davie and his wife, Elspeth, who lived on the opposite side of the street. George was a lecturer in philosophy and a great intellectual force. Elspeth was a calm personality, intelligent and charming, and an accomplished stylist in novels and short stories. I met George frequently because he was a regular attender at social events concerned with the intellectual life of Edinburgh. Whenever you met him he would launch at once without preliminary chatter into a Socratic dialogue as if we had never parted since the last time. His important book, *The Democratic Intellect,* was a powerful argument for the Scottish tradition of a wide approach to education and against the premature specialisation, which had been imported from England.

I first met Robin Jenkins when he came to Edinburgh in the 1980s and 90s to give readings in the admirable programmes which the Saltire Society used to present during the Edinburgh Festival. He had an ability to give more wit and point to extracts from his own novels than was immediately apparent when you first read them. I last met him when Ian Arnott, Douglas Gifford and I went in 2001 to present him with the Andrew Fletcher award from the Saltire Society at his incredibly remote and isolated house in the southern end of the Cowal peninsula. He had been living alone there since the death of his wife. When I asked him why he had chosen it, he said it was because of the view. This was not apparent from the ground floor, but from the floor above, I saw the point, a splendid vista of the entrance to the Firth of Clyde. He had travelled extensively. Indeed when I was in South East Asia department of the Foreign Office I had put him in touch with the British Council for a teaching post in Afghanistan. Even so, his thoughts and most of his novels were firmly based in Scotland. There were many things about contemporary life which disturbed him, but he had a basic cheerfulness which constantly broke through.

In the early 80s I used to meet Allan Massie quite frequently, but hardly at all since he retired, like Walter Scott, to live in the Borders in a house near Bowhill. I visited him there once or twice. Apart from his novels he has been an incredibly prolific commentator on all sorts of subjects in the Scottish and London press. We have disputed at times in print, but I think that we agree on many things more intellectually than instinctively. He wrote a charming and modest account of his life for *Spirits of the Age*. He says in it that he is 'out of the mainstream of contemporary Scottish writing'. That is true in a way, but he is one of our best living novelists who has also written an astonishing amount of intelligent comment on a vast range of subjects.

I have known Alasdair Gray since his first, and epoch-making novel, *Lanark,* was published by Canongate in 1981. As I mentioned in the autobiography, he disappeared at the launch after a lavish introduction by the publisher. Sometimes on public occasions his shyness has made him behave rather absurdly. A few minutes conversation with him soon reveals that he is a man of very wide reading and impressive intellect. He is a painter too, of course. In 2006 he painted a portrait of Laura and myself. I thought that it made us both look rather gloomy and not on very good terms with one another. Alasdair said that he thought that it revealed me as a profound thinker. I was not convinced.

I first met James Robertson when we were both members of the Committee of Scottish PEN and also at meetings of the Sir Walter Scott Club. He is another fine novelist, worthy of comparison in the treatment of history with Sir Walter himself. Both he and his wife, Marianne, are splendid company. In his essay in *Spirits of the Age*, he says that 'MacDiarmid started a revolution in my head'. I think that this is true of Scotland as a whole, although most people are not conscious of it. He speaks too of his response to Scots, again something which I share. He and Matthew Fitt have done great work for Scots through their books for children in the *Itchy Coo* series.

Joan Lingard is another accomplished and prolific novelist and good company. I first met her too through PEN and her campaigning against nuclear weapons and the nuclear submarines on the Clyde.

Alexander McCall Smith was a member of the Committee of Scottish PEN when I was the President and we were preparing for an International PEN Congress in Edinburgh. Before that time he also edited the PEN Newsletter for some years. At the same time he was a professor of Medical Law in Edinburgh University and his publications were academic books on that subject, although I think that he was already working on novels based on his youthful experiences in Botswana. In a harsh world Sandy is a model of decency, modesty, charm and kindness. He is still the same, absolutely unspoilt by his enormous success as a worldwide best seller. When this first began to happen I ran into him at the Edinburgh Book Festival and told him how pleased I was to hear of it, he was so lavish in his thanks for my kindness in saying so that you might think that I had been responsible.

Although I was a distant member of the SNP for many years, and a supporter since my school days, I was only able to become directly involved when I came back to Edinburgh in 1980. Since then I have been a member of the Edinburgh Branch, for several years a Vice-President of the party and a member of the National Executive Committee and a constant delegate to the National Council and to the annual Conference. At all of them I have made many friends. The SNP has had the advantage of bringing together people with an affection for Scotland and an intellectual conviction of the need for independence. For years many people have devoted effort, time and money to it with only very little visible progress. The British state, with its formidable propaganda machine and centuries of experience in political manipulation, has resisted stubbornly. In response the members of the SNP have developed habits of intellectual conviction and patience tempered by optimism.

Among them, of course, the outstanding figure is Alex Salmond, whom I have valued as a friend for more than twenty years. He wrote generous revues of my autobiography in which he said that I had been 'a whirlwind of positive activity in the intellectual life of the nation. . . with a continuing ability to bowl a googly and spring a surprise'. We had held a joint discussion about the book at the SNP Conference in October 2002 and Alex wrote to me in November to suggest that we should do this again in Duff House. This is an outpost of the National Gallery of Scotland in Banff, not far from Alex's house in Strichen. The custodian, or Chamberlain to give him his official title, was my old friend and colleague from the Montreal Exhibition in 1967, Charles Burnett. Since then, in addition to his post in Banff, he has become the Rothesay Herald. I have met him from time to time, usually in the New Club, when he has been attending some ceremony in his heraldic finery. Alex sent me a copy of his letter to Burnett in which he used the surprising phrase that I was 'a jewel in our midst'.

This discussion duly took place in December. Alex and Moira handsomely entertained Laura and me afterwards in the mill house in Strichen which they were in the process of converting into an impregnable retreat from the pressures of the outside world. In fact, Moira has always displayed an impressive ability to keep them at safe distance.

In the last few years Harry Reid has become one of my most valued friends. He has been living fairly constantly in his Edinburgh house since he retired from the editorship of *The Herald*. He is a man of wide knowledge of the world, strong ideas and powers of expression. We agree about most things, including Scottish independence, with two important exceptions, football and the church. I think that the time spent by many people, not to mention the press and broadcasters, on professional football is an absurd waste of time and energy. It has become one of the worst examples of commercialised indulgence and greed on one side and exploitation on the other. I can see nothing pleasant and interesting in it as a spectacle. Harry has the excuse that he was once a sports writer, and I think sports editor, of *The Scotsman*.

Religion too is something which I deplore. I think that it is an insult to human intelligence that people should still profess to believe in ideas evolved many centuries ago such as the existence of god or gods and life after death. After all this time there is not a scrap of evidence to support anything so basically improbable and contrary to all experience. Churches have been so firmly established with an aura of dignity and importance about them that even now they are able to radiate an atmosphere of superiority to criticism. That atmosphere was able to restrain even David Hume from expressing himself freely. At that time, the Kirk in Scotland was so dominant in the life of the country that it was beyond challenge. Have we made no progress since the first wave of the Enlightenment?

Religion, although often on the side of virtue and kindness, has often been and still is a major cause of wars, oppression and violence. This applies even between different wings of the same religion. It was so, until very recently in Northern Ireland between two branches of Christianity. It is so between Sunni and Shi-ite in Iraq as well as between extremist Islam and the West.

Now I admit that the Church of Scotland, to which Harry belongs and about which he has written an important book, is remarkably free from most of the evils of religious extremity. It has been democratic in structure long before the State and so free from dogmatism that it has no machinery except an annual assembly to issue statements on current issues. On the whole, it has been a force for good in Scottish life with its influence on rigorous morality, effort and thought. Above all, since the time of John Knox, his insistence on the importance of education has been of immense value to Scotland. Harry has said that I was a useful source for his book. Perhaps after all our views on this subject are not so far apart.

I must admit too that Harry has made some very generous remarks about me in print. In 1990, along with Arnold Kemp, he edited *The Herald Book of Scotland*. Harry contributed an essay to it, *The Auld Enemy: Scotland and England*, in which he said: 'Paul Scott is one of the most interesting men now living in Scotland, and somebody who should be much better known in our country.' On 24th April 1989 the first leader in *The Herald*, which I think was probably written by Harry, was headed 'Significant Rectorial Address'. It discussed the address which I was due to give that evening when I was installed as Rector of Dundee University. 'Mr Scott,' it said, 'in indicting the Government, is also seeking to move the debate onto higher ground. He will, in effect, be calling for a new Scottish Enlightenment. This is portentous stuff.' Christopher Harvie telephoned me from Tübingen to say that it was probably the first time since the days of Carlyle that so much attention had been paid to a Rectorial Address.

I think that it was also Harry Reid who told me that Neal Ascherson, who at that time worked at *The Scotsman* as Harry did himself, had been spreading the idea that I had returned to Scotland in 1980 as some sort of government secret agent. Harry mentioned this in a Profile of me which he wrote in *The Herald* of 10th September 1990: 'It was whispered in the political and literary *demi-monde* of Edinburgh that Scott was in fact a spy acting for HM Government – or even worse an *agent provocateur*.'

I was astonished when Harry told me, although he did not mention it in the Profile, that Ascherson was the source of this absurd story. I had met him when he called to see me in Milan some years before and I had read many of his articles and books. I had the impression that he was highly intelligent and well informed about current affairs and the ways of the world. How could he possibly believe such nonsense?

As is evident from the Foreign Office personnel reports which I have quoted in chapter 1, I never concealed my strong commitment to Scotland during my diplomatic career. Nor was I alone among my colleagues. There were many Scots among them and we sometimes discussed how much we would enjoy working one of these days in a Scottish Foreign Office in Edinburgh. There was no secret about my opinion on such matters.

I saw no sign myself that anyone took Ascherson's fantasy seriously. In fact, I see from my diary that Harry Reid himself told me in November 2002 that 'my return to Scotland in 1980 had a wonderful and invigorating effect on the situation in the country'. I suspected myself that some people wondered what right I had suddenly to emerge from abroad and start expressing views on the Scottish situation and take initiatives to change it. Indeed I am sometimes astonished myself to realise that I was able within a year or two of my return to Scotland in 1980 to start such things as the Advisory Council for the Arts in Scotland

(AdCAS), the Saltire Book Awards and a new campaign to establish a Scottish National Theatre. Of course, in all of these I had great help from my colleagues in the Saltire Society.

In his recent book, *The Road to Independence*, Murray Pittock says that AdCAS 'managed to make itself heard in government circles' and that several of our objectives were achieved even under a Conservative Government such as a separate Scottish Arts Council and a Scottish Higher Education Funding Council. The National Theatre followed under Labour. I was also delighted that we were able to persuade the Scottish Arts Council to sponsor paperback reprints of important Scottish books from all periods. The publisher, Canongate, in particular responded with a comprehensive series of classics from the fourteenth century to the present, many of which had been out of print for years. We were able to persuade two Directors of the Edinburgh Festival, Frank Dunlop and Brian MacMaster, to include more Scottish work in their programmes. Frank promoted the admirable Saltire Society programmes in the Fringe to the Festival itself. AdCAS was launched in 1981 and came to an end in 1999 when a majority of its member organisations decided, perhaps with too much optimism, that the recovery of the Scottish Parliament made it unnecessary.

The Saltire Society itself continued of course to do valuable work. We were able, for instance, to arrange for the permanent display in its ideal location, Smailholm Tower, of the beautiful figures by Anne Carrick of characters from many of the Border Ballads. This became possible when Ian Gilmour and his wife, Meta Forrest, provided funds from 'an anonymous donor' to purchase the entire collection. For years Meta and Ian produced the admirable Saltire Society programmes in the Edinburgh Fringe and eventually in the Festival itself of Scottish literature and music. Their own contribution, as unequalled performers of poetry and prose mainly in Scots, was an impressive part of these events. They both died a few years ago, and no one has yet replaced them.

No less than James Halliday, a former Chairman of the SNP

and a stalwart campaigner, confessed in a review in the *Scots Independent* in August 1991 of my book, *Towards Independence*, to sharing 'a furtive feeling of resentment' when people arrive from abroad and 'appear to be teaching their grandmothers to suck eggs'. He then said in his review:

> I cherished some such feelings as I read Paul Scott's contributions during the years since his retirement and return to permanent residence in Scotland. I now wish, very publicly and most sincerely, to beg his pardon for my doubts and grudges, because he has, in this collection done the finest service to the national intellectual cause which has appeared, in my judgement, in my life time.

> Of course the case is not new, but its consolidated present-ation is, and it is presented with enormous grace and clarity. His skills have earned for him the respect and attention of the literary and intellectual world and, because of this, people of position and influence read and reflect upon what he says to a degree which they never did before. That for our cause, is pure gain.

Halliday goes on to discuss one of my essays in *Towards Independence*, 'Severitas, the Roman-Scottish Ideal', which appeared originally in *Blackwood's Magazine* of November 1976. It discussed the Scottish aspiration to adopt this Roman virtue, 'being severe with oneself', along with respect for the intellect and education. Halliday doubts if this ideal was ever widely accepted and sees very few signs of it today, although he thinks that it may linger in middle-class Edinburgh.

> The more that education in Scotland has become a blend of hedonism and utility, presenting words like 'academic' and 'intellectual' as terms of abuse, the less has been any general commitment to the qualities which Scott admires.

It is certainly true that the present fashion for 'dumbing down' and superficial absurdity is the opposite of the old ideal and that is a sad decline. I was not conscious of any deliberate indoctrination in my youth. Perhaps we absorbed it unconsciously in the atmosphere of the place and of the old High School of Edinburgh. As Sydney Smith wrote to Jeffrey in 1819, 'You must consider that Edinburgh is a very grave place and that you live with Philosophers who are very intolerant of nonsense.' We could now do with more of that spirit.

Another of my friends who, like Harry Reid, has strong connections with the Kirk is Ian Campbell. Indeed he plays the organ in church on Sundays. His father was a Church of Scotland minister who at one time was in charge of the Scottish church in Geneva. That was where Ian was born and it has made him a lifelong enthusiast for Switzerland, one of the feelings we share. He has been for some years, and is now about to retire, Professor of Scottish and Victorian Literature (a strange combination) in Edinburgh University. That is where I first met him in the early 1980s when I did a postgraduate course in Scottish literature. He is full of enthusiasm, erudition and ideas about his subject and is a brilliant lecturer. Since he also retains an air of youthfulness and is a very hospitable bachelor it is not surprising that he is very popular with his students. One of his enthusiasms, which I find a little strange, is for Thomas Carlyle. He has written a book about him and he is one of the editors of the forty or so volumes of the admittedly fascinating letters of Thomas and his wife, Jane Welsh. Ian is also the master spirit of a Carlyle Society which meets frequently during the winter and to which I was persuaded to lecture recently.

Also not long ago Laura and I were at Tom Devine's inaugural lecture as Professor of Scottish History in Edinburgh University. Billy Kay, a fellow campaigner for the Scots language, sat beside us and, in the course of reminiscing about his student days, happened to mention how much he had enjoyed Ian Campbell's lectures. And, he said, he took them on a fascinating expedition to the country of Lewis Grassic Gibbon's *Sunset Song*, another of Ian's enthusiasms. It culminated with tea in the manse with the minister who was Ian's father.

Iain Gordon Brown of the National Library and his wife, Patricia, are among the other great assets of Edinburgh life whose company is both a pleasure and an intellectual stimulus. He is an authority on many aspects of Scottish life, including Walter Scott, Clerk of Penicuik and the history of Edinburgh.

Of course, it is Laura who for the last thirty years or so has been my closest ally and indispensable companion. Indeed because of an accident on 9th September 2006, which I call in my diary 'a minor disaster', I could hardly have survived without her. The accident was, as so often, rather absurd. Since we no longer have a car and it is difficult to visit such places as National Trust properties without one, we went with a bus party to visit Hill House in Helensburgh. On the return journey we stopped for tea in Drymen. I assumed that the bus was parked on a flat road, but it was in fact on an embankment with a strong list to starboard. So when I opened the side door, because I happened to be sitting close to it, the door flew open and projected me into space. I landed violently on a hard pavement and found that I could not move. An ambulance took me to the Infirmary in Stirling and after a few days I was transferred to Edinburgh. They diagnosed a fracture of the left acetabulum, something I had never heard of, but it is a bowl-shaped bone at the top of the leg.

I was released from the Infirmary on 3rd October 2006, but now, more than a year later, I still cannot walk or stand, even with a stick, for more than a few minutes without pain. This is not only because of the effect of the accident. For some years I have had a problem now and again with my left knee. Also in 2005 I started to have an acute pain, when I walked, at the top of my right leg. This was diagnosed in October of that year as the mysterious consequence of pressure on a nerve in my spine, lumbar canal stenosis in medical language. In May 2006 I had to cancel our reservation for the flat in Klosters to ski in January 2007. Laura and I have been going to Klosters to ski every year since the late 1970s and for over twenty years we rented the basement flat of Frau Crameri with a fine view of the mountains. When that became unavailable we found another that was even more convenient. I have skied every winter since the Army introduced me to it in the Cairngorms in 1942 when we were preparing, or pretending to prepare, for an invasion of Norway.

But I have no right to complain. I have been skiing until January 2006 and still, I am told , fluently and swiftly. Not many people are fortunate enough still to be skiing at the age of 85. Strangely enough, I remember thinking years ago that I would like to be able to ski until I was 85 and then retire gracefully from it.

I hope that David Hume was right when he said in *A Treatise of Human Nature:* 'We are no sooner acquainted with the impossibility of satisfying any desire than the desire itself vanishes'. In my experience this has been true of sailing. For years I was devoted to it and spent much of my free time in my dingy on the Thames at Hammersmith or in my Dragon on the St.Lawrence in Montreal. In Milan there was no opportunity for such an indulgence and I found, as Hume says, that the desire itself vanished.

I hope for some improvement, and there has been a little, but now for about a year there are many simple things that I cannot do without help, such as walking to the bus stop or the local shops. I can still attend (or give) lectures, theatres, concerts and committee meetings and the like, as long as someone gives me a lift or I take a taxi. I can go round exhibitions, especially if I can borrow a wheelchair. Also receptions if there is somewhere to sit, but to be left sitting in splendid isolation is not much of a pleasure. There is no point in going to such places as Paris or Vienna or visiting great country houses and the like if you can't wander about. So, despite the views of David Hume, I should still prefer to be able to walk and stand normally.

Up to now I have not really felt old, but now staggering about with a stick I must look like it. I have really been very fortunate for most of my life. I have had no serious illness, except appendicitis when I was at school. Even now, I have many reasons to enjoy life. We have a comfortable place to live, a fine view, pictures on the walls and thousands of books. I agree with Edward Gibbon when he says in his *Autobiography* that his 'numerous and select library is the foundation of his works and the best comfort of his life.' If I can't go out, I have more time to read and write.

But all of this is only possible because of Laura. She is a constant encouragement and indispensable help. She runs the household impeccably and comes with me to help me to move whenever I venture out. In addition to all of that she manages the e-mails, an institution which is sometimes helpful but more often a pest. She transfers many of my handwritten drafts (which few other people could read) to the computer. Harry Reid said that she is a wonderful woman and that is certainly true.

Handwritten drafts in this day and age? Yes, I confess that it is my habit and addiction. I think more readily with a pen in my hand than with a keyboard at my finger tips. In fact, I think I spend as much time sitting at my desk writing as I did when I was working in the Foreign Office. I have a constant urge to write. The subject is usually Scottish because the fascination of its past and the problems and opportunities of the exciting present are inescapable.

At about the time when my autobiography was about to be published I was working with George Bruce on a new edition of *A Scottish Postbag* of which we had edited the first edition in 1986. At that time we had enormous pleasure of hunting for letters from the days of Wallace to Sorley Maclean which said something interesting and said it with eloquence or wit. The result, I think, was a very lively book and a good introduction to Scottish history and to the people who made it or wrote about it. George was very enthusiastic about the book and called it 'a minor classic'.

I cannot remember who suggested that we should produce a new edition with additional letters from the last twenty years or so, but by that time George was in his 90s. That did not deter him. He had, after all, recently won the Saltire Award for the Scottish Book of the Year for his latest collection of poetry. It was evident that he no longer had the same vigour and instant response to ideas, but he had plenty of go and spirit for all that. It was a sad blow when he died just as the new edition was going to press. We had been close colleagues in diverse Saltire Society activities for more than twenty years, especially in the Publications Committee and in the Saltire programmes in the Edinburgh Festival Fringe and ultimately in the Festival itself. He was a constant source of sharp, intelligent and useful comment and advice.

Shortly after George died, the editor of the *Oxford Dictionary of National Biography* wrote to ask me to write an entry on him. By this time the new *ODNB* had already appeared in print in many volumes. I had contributed the entries on John Galt and one or two others. Now new entries, such as that on George, would be available only on the web, until eventually supplements are printed. The Research Editor, Alex May, wrote to me about my entry on George:

> The article is exactly the kind of thing we were hoping for, but all too rarely get: nicely judged, elegantly written, comprehensive in its coverage of Bruce's career and achievements as a poet and broadcaster, and conveying a real sense of his significance in relation to the Scottish Renaissance and Scottish culture more generally.

This new *ODNB*, like its predecessors, but on an even larger scale, is an impressive and thorough work of scholarship to which a great many people have contributed. Normally it can be regarded as a reliable source for the available information about its subjects and quoted as an authority. It was therefore shocking to read the entry on Andrew Fletcher of Saltoun, the robust defender of Scottish independence in the Scottish Parliament from 1703 to 1707. It is by John Robertson, a Scot from Edinburgh who teaches modern history at Oxford. He reaches the absurd conclusion that Fletcher 'was not a champion of Scottish independence' on the grounds that his name was linked with John Trinchard and Daniel Defoe by an anonymous writer in a Glasgow newspaper of 1840. I wrote to the Editor in protest, but now that it is in print there is not much that they can do about it. The entry will no doubt startle and confuse readers for years to come.

Since I came back to Edinburgh, in November 1980, I have written a fairly steady flow of what might be called essays for the newspapers and magazines. They deal mostly with literary, historical, or political subjects, and again are mostly about Scotland. Over the years I have published four collections of them: *Towards Independence* (Polygon, 1991, and Saltire 1996); *Defoe in Edinburgh and other Papers* (Tuckwell Press, 1995); *Still in Bed with an Elephant* (Saltire, 1998) and *Scotland Resurgent* (Saltire 2003). Another is about to be published, *The Age of Liberation* (Saltire) a title which refers to the present age in which the submerged nations within the Empires and most of the multi-national states have reasserted their freedom, an example which I hope Scotland will shortly follow.

I have written a steady flow of book reviews, mostly for *The Scotsman* and the *Sunday Herald*. For many years I wrote reviews of the Edinburgh Fringe for *The Scotsman* and of the Festival for *The Economist* and of both for BBC Radio Scotland.

In these last seven years I have edited two collections of works by other people. *The Saltoun Papers* (Saltire 2003) was of the lectures (including one of my own) given over the years in East Saltoun annually in September in commemoration of Andrew Fletcher. In 2006 the event was transferred to the building of the Scottish Parliament. I was due to give the first of these, but since I was in hospital following my accident, it was read by Ian Scott. Then in 2005 I edited *Spirits of the Age: Scottish Self-Portraits* (Saltire), a collection of autobiographical essays which I persuaded many of the influential Scots of the time to write.

In the last few years Laura and I have been going on cruises as a direct consequence of our membership of Scottish PEN. In 1987 we went to our first PEN International Congress in Lugano. There we became acquainted with Lucia Ambrogini of the Swiss-Italian PEN Centre who were the organisers of the event. She persuaded us to join a party she was arranging to go on a cruise in the following year with the Italian Costa Line from Venice to the Greek Islands and Istanbul. We enjoyed this so much that we next went on a Ukrainian ship from Tilbury to the Baltic. It was then that we discovered that better things were available in the cruises of Swan Hellenic and the National Trust for Scotland on the *Black Prince* of the Fred Olsen Line. They were better mainly in the sense that they had intelligent programmes on board of music and lectures. We went twice with Swan Hellenic, to the Black Sea and round Italy. On the *Black Prince* we had many cruises, to Iceland, the Norwegian fjords and Spitzbergen, Orkney and Shetland, the Hebrides, Ireland, Spain and France (where I achieved a long held wish to visit the tower of Montaigne) and to all the countries of the Baltic.

These experiences had two results. I began to be appointed as one of the lecturers and I began to research the activities of Scots in Norway and the Baltic countries mainly in the sixteenth and seventeenth centuries. My cruise lecturing began when I happened to read Walter Scott's *Journal* of his voyage to Orkney, Shetland and the Hebrides in the yacht of the Commissioners of the Northern Lights. I suggested to Anne Campbell, who was in charge of the National Trust cruises, that it would be a good idea to have a cruise which followed the same route. Not long afterwards she wrote to me to say that they would do that and would I join them as a lecturer. That was in 2003 and since then I have lectured on many cruises, mainly to Norway and the countries of the Baltic.

The Scottish contribution to these countries is a fascinating story. For instance, Norway's greatest composer, Edvard Grieg, and the first important modern writer in Norwegian, Petter Dass, were both the sons of Scots who settled in Norway. When Gustavus Adolphus made Sweden a European power in the seventeenth century, about seventy of his senior officers were Scots. So too was his Minister of War, Alexander Erskine, who represented Sweden at the conference which made the Peace of Westphalia. There are many other examples in European history of Scots being entrusted with important diplomatic missions on behalf of other countries.

In 1651, when he was 15, Patrick Gordon left Aberdeen to seek his fortune in Europe. He was recruited into the Swedish army by an officer who praised Scotland by saying that there is no better soldier than Scots because 'nature had endowed them with a genius fit for anything.' This may have been calculated flattery, but it seems to have been a view widely held in Europe at the time. Within a few years, Moscow and Vienna were competing for Gordon's services. He chose Moscow and within a few years he was head of the Russian army and a close friend of the Czar, Peter the Great. The historian, Hill Burton, said of Patrick Gordon: 'After his friend and master, Peter the Great, it may be questioned if any other one man did so much for the early consolidation of the Russian Empire'.

In recent years there has been a wide recognition that Scots have made a remarkable contribution in many parts of the world. Christopher Harvie in his book *Scotland and Nationalism* in 1977 said: 'The Scots have probably done more to create the modern world than any other nation. They owe it an explanation.'

The American Arthur Herman in *The Scottish Enlightenment: The Scots Invention of the Modern World* (2002) agrees:

> A new social ethos was born, which the rest of the world
> would come to see as quintessentially American – and
> quintessentially modern. In fact it is quintessentially
> Scottish. . . As the first modern nation and culture, the
> Scots have by and large made the world a better place.

He recognised that the British Empire was 'largely built and organised by Scots' and that we were 'the dominant influence' in Canada and Australia.

Herman's book shows that he has made a close study of Scottish history from the eighteenth century onwards, but evidently not of the earlier period. He says that Scotland had a 'barbarous history' – as if the Enlightenment had sprung out of nothing instead of several centuries of philosophy. He has been challenged on this by two other Americans, A.L.Blieforth and R.J.Munro in their book, *The Scottish Invention of America, Democracy and Human Rights* (2004). They argue that there has been a consistent development of the idea that government should rest on the consent of the governed from Gaelic tradition, Duns Scotus in the thirteenth century, the Declaration of Arbroath and the writings of John Major, George Buchanan and John Knox. They also quote from Francis Hutcheson to show the close similarity between his words and those used by Thomas Jefferson in the Declaration of Independence some fifty years later, both about the rights of the people and the pursuit of happiness. They are convinced that the ideas behind the American Declaration had their origin in Scotland.

These are only a few examples, but there is clear evidence that in the seventeenth and eighteenth centuries in Europe, and subsequently in America, the Scots had a high reputation for intelligence, skill and reliability. Lord Macaulay in his *History of England* (Edition of 1858, Vol.IV, pp 82-83) offers an explanation. He writes of the effect of the Education Act passed by the Scottish Parliament in 1695, although the emphasis on education in Scotland had begun more than a century before with John Knox's *Book of Discipline*:

> It began to be evident that the common people of
> Scotland were superior in intelligence to the common
> people of any country in Europe. . . Scotland made good
> progress in all that constitutes civilisation, as the Old
> World had never seen equalled, and even the new World
> has scarcely seen surpassed. This wonderful change is to
> be attributed, not indeed solely, but principally, to the
> national system of education.

Many other people have commented on the quality and effect of Scottish education. Two examples. Kunston Loch-Szyrma was in Scotland from 1820 to 1826 as tutor of two Polish princes. He travelled widely in the country and met many people including Walter Scott, James Hogg and Dugald Stewart. In his *Reminiscences* he said:

> The high educational standards and the iron endeavour of the Scots will be surpassed by no one. . . There is certainly no country in which education is so much cared for as in Scotland. . . This is why everything a Scot does is always sensible and well thought out.

And Arthur Herman in the book which I have mentioned:

> In no other European country did education count for so much, or enjoy so broad a base. . . No other society in Europe was so broadly prepared for take off into the modern age as was eighteenth century Scotland.

In addition to the cruises and skiing (until 2006 that is) we were enticed abroad by two other things. In 1997 I went for the first time to an annual meeting of writers which Slovenian PEN holds in a splendid hotel on the shores of Lake Bled. This must be one of the most beautiful places in Europe. The lake itself is magnificent, surrounded by densely wooded country in the foothills of the Alps with snow-covered peaks in the distance; a baroque church on an island in the middle of the lake and a fairytale castle on a projecting rock above. Marshall Tito showed his appreciation of the fine things in life by having a residence there which is now a hotel where the PEN meetings always have one of the receptions.

But even all of that is the least of it. It is the character of the Slovenes themselves that makes these conferences so worthwhile. They are friendly, warm and enthusiastic and arrange debates on subjects often of particular relevance to small countries, like

Slovenia and Scotland. I usually write a paper for these discussions each year.

Another fascinating thing about Bled has been to witness the response of the Slovenes to their newly acquired independence. The rapid emergence of self-confidence, delight in their new status, and increase in prosperity, has been fascinating to observe.

At first I went alone, but since Laura has retired from her job in the Italian Consulate-General, but is still active in PEN, she has joined me each year. We normally go there by train to Ljubljana from Venice, which gives us an opportunity to spend a day or two in that incomparable place, usually in our favourite (but very expensive) hotel, the Monaco & Grand Canal. Even when I cannot walk, I can still get around in Venice by vaporetto.

This travel is a consequence of our acquisition of a small, but delightful, flat in the small town of Acqui Terme in the southern hills of the region of Piedmont, in Italy, in easy reach of Genoa, Turin and Milan. This is the part of the world where Laura's grandparents lived, where she spent her summer holidays as a schoolgirl and to which her parents retired. While they were alive we used to visit them there. We soon realised after they died it was not practicable to maintain their large flat for occasional visits from Edinburgh, but Laura wanted to keep a foothold in this place of which she had such memories. In October 2003 we found the ideal solution. It is in a modern building, on the two top floors, 6th and 7th, with a lift and a spacious balcony. There is a street with cars at the side, but at the front an open large lawn surrounded by very high poplars. There is a fine view of a hill – all of this although it is quite close to the centre of the town and the railway station.

Acqui Terme itself is an interesting place. Anywhere but in Italy, which is so rich in splendours, it would be famous. As its name suggests, it has a hot and cold springs discovered, of course, by the Romans (who seem to have found all of them in Europe). It is still in use and treatments in it, mud baths and the like, are one of the local industries. I have been wondering if they would do some good to my legs. There are still remaining three arches of a Roman acqueduct. The town is still old-fashioned enough to have a variety of small specialist shops run by people who know and care about the things they sell. After the turmoil of Edinburgh, it is peace, perfect peace.

All this gadding about does not mean that I neglect my work. I read and reviewed three substantial books while I was in the Edinburgh Infirmary. Whenever I go I always take books and pen and paper. I have written most of the present book in two weeks or so in the summer of 2007 in Acqui. And, of course, there is now the convenience and curse of a steady flow of e-mail messages. It is useful to be kept in touch, but there are times when I feel that this invention is one of the major torments of modern life.

I see from my diary that I told Neil MacCormick in September 2003 that I was sorry to see that he had decided not to stand for a second term as an SNP member of the European Parliament. He said that he was sorry too, but the older he was, the more he regretted spending time out of Scotland. I feel that as well. I always leave Edinburgh with hesitation and return with relief and pleasure. That does not mean that I do not enjoy my forays abroad and they have their own particular pleasures and advantages. Also Laura has, of course, as much right as me to want to spend time in a place which has special associations for her as I have in Edinburgh. In addition, Edinburgh and Acqui are a delightful combination of opposites.

•

May 2007 was not only the month of the third election to the Scottish Parliament, but of the tercentenary of the Treaty of Union which came into force on 1st May 1707. At that time there were triumphant celebrations in London, but only apprehension and anxiety in Edinburgh. In 2007 there was no official celebration, That was not surprising because the way in which the Union came about was not very creditable to either country. As Hume Brown, said of it: 'A people does not gladly turn its eyes to a period when its representative men. . . compromise the national character in the eyes of the world.' England did not want to be seen as a larger country forcing its will on a smaller one; Scotland as succumbing to bribery and a threat of invasion.

But if there was no celebration, there was a considerable amount of public debate. This involved three of us who had written books on the subject, Christopher Whatley, Michael Fry and myself. We had in fact our first public encounter in a discussion at a conference in Edinburgh in July 2002 of the Eighteenth Century Scottish Studies Society. In 2007 we had such debates in the National Library, the National Gallery, the Museum of Scotland, the Royal Society of Edinburgh and the Edinburgh International Book Festival as well as the radio and television. The striking thing about these debates is the extent to which people familiar with the same set of facts can reach quite different conclusions about them. We are all liable to be influenced by extraneous preferences and ideas. Attitudes to the Union are an interesting example.

In the eighteenth century the immediate effect of the Union was to depress Scottish trade for several decades, as Daniel Defoe was sorry to discover when he made his tour in the 1720s. Apart from the suppression of the Jacobites and of Highland society, the Parliament in London took very little interest in Scotland and when it did it was not very helpful. It introduced patronage into the Church of Scotland, which lead to the disaster of the Disruption in 1843. Otherwise Scotland was very much left, as Walter Scott said in the *Malachi Letters*, 'to win her silent way to national wealth and consequence'.

During the period there was very little doubt in Scotland about the way in which the Union had come about. To quote Walter Scott again, and he was, of course, well informed about these comparatively recent events:

Men of whom a majority had thus been bought and sold,

forfeited every right to interfere in the terms which
England insisted upon. . . But despised by the English,
and detested by their own country. . . had no alternative
left save that of following the unworthy bargain they had
made. . . a total surrender of their independence, by their
false and corrupted statesmen into the hand of their
proud and powerful rival.

This was the accepted view of the nature of the Union until
about the middle of the nineteenth century, or until the existence
of the British Empire began to have a major impact on Scotland.
Thousands of Scots made brilliant careers in its administration.
It was a valuable source of raw materials for Scottish industry
and a market for their exports. Now it is a period of which we
tend to feel ashamed because of its dependence on the slave
trade and the exploitation of the local populations. By what
right did Europeans assume the government of these distant
territories? At the time, however, it was a source of pride. By
virtue of it Britain was a world power and we believed that we
were spreading civilisation, progress and Christianity in
primitive and previously underdeveloped parts of the world.
Scotland was a partner in this enterprise by virtue of the Union
and this meant that there was an urge to take a favourable view
of the Union itself and of the people who made it.

The theory became established that Scotland (or the few
people in the Scottish Parliament who decided such matters in
a completely undemocratic age) wanted the Union to escape
from the consequences of the Darien disaster and achieve access
to trade with the English colonies. This sounds plausible because
of what happened many years later, but it was not how it seemed
at the time. In 1707 very few people in Scotland thought about
trade with the colonies. As Adam Smith said of the Union in a
letter in 1760:

The immediate effect of it was to hurt the interest of every
single order of men in the country. . . Even the merchants

seemed to suffer at first. The trade to the plantations was, indeed, opened to them. But that was a trade which they know nothing about; the trade they were acquainted with, that of France, Holland and the Baltic, was laid under new embarrassments which almost totally annihilated the two first and most important branches of it. . . . No wonder if at that time all orders of men conspired in cursing a measure so hurtful to their immediate interest.

As for Darien, King William in response to an appeal by both Houses of the English Parliament did his best to frustrate it particularly by preventing the raising of capital in the London and European markets. The entire amount was raised in Scotland by a great patriotic endeavour in which many Scots, including members of Parliament, invested all they could afford. They thought that they had lost all of it. This helped to bring about the Union in the sense that it gave an opportunity to the English Government, as one of their most potent forms of bribery, to offer (or rather pretend to offer) in the terms of the Treaty itself the repayment of these losses.

The plausible, but unhistorical view of the Union, was so thoroughly established that it has become the orthodox view even among normally well informed academics. It is at the root of all these debates in which I have been involved. But, of course, this is distant history and what matters at present is what we should do about the Union now. This was one of the principal issues of the Scottish Election in May 2007 to which I turn in the next chapter. ❏

5. Dawn At Last

For several weeks before the Election for the Scottish Parliament on Thursday 3rd May 2007 opinion polls had shown a clear lead for the SNP, but the traditional support for the Labour Party seemed to rally towards the end of the campaign. There was appalling confusion at the count with an unprecedented deluge of spoiled papers. This was generally blamed on a change in their design. I was astonished to hear afterwards that the change had been decided in London not Edinburgh. Westminster is evidently still anxious to assert control.

We were still uncertain about the final result when we arrived at an SNP celebration in the Hub, the Edinburgh Festival HQ in the High Street, at about 5pm on the Friday. There we were met by a triumphant Michael Hance outside the building who told us that the news of the final count had just come through. The SNP were the largest party by one seat more than Labour. Naturally the atmosphere in the Hub was jubilant. Alex Salmond made an enthusiastic speech.

There was some doubt in the next few days about the formation of the Government. The Liberal-Democrats, who were in third position, were adamant that they would not form a coalition with the SNP, or even meet to discuss the possibility, unless we dropped the commitment to hold a referendum on independence, a curious position for professed liberals. At the same time, they and the other unionist parties said that they were certain that the majority of Scots did not want independence. Why then were they so unwilling to put it to a vote?

It soon emerged that the Liberal-Democrats were also not prepared to renew their coalition with Labour. The Conservatives stood apart. The SNP negotiated an understanding with the two members of the Green Party. Alex Salmond was duly elected as First Minister and the SNP, after about seventy years of patient endeavour, was now at last the party of Government in Scotland and the fifty years of Labour domination was at an end.

By the time that the SNP National Council met, in that absurd building, Dynamic Earth, in Edinburgh on 23rd June the Government was already thoroughly established. Alex and all the ministers around him had already shown their obvious superiority to their predecessors in every respect. They were all old friends, people with whom I had sat many times round the table at meetings of the National Executive Committee of the party. Talk about friends in high places! They now form the whole government.

The National Council meeting, which I attended as a delegate from the Edinburgh Branch, radiated satisfaction and optimism. I remarked to John Swinney about the obvious transformation of the Cabinet and the Parliament. Ministerial statements and the debates were now worth listening to. This must be obvious to anyone who watches the TV coverage and it must be winning new support for the SNP. He agreed and said that, because of it, he was sure that people would be outraged if the opposition parties staged some sort of parliamentary conspiracy against the SNP government. Alex Salmond told me that he would speak to Fiona Hyslop and Linda Fabiani to see if I could help with cultural policy. I have had brief conversations with both of them at social events recently and I have met them both as part of a delegation from the Saltire Society.

As I write, the SNP Government have been in office for just over a year and in that time they have already achieved many of their manifesto commitments. Alex Salmond has adjusted to the conduct of a Government without a majority in Parliament with impeccable skill. His whole ministerial team are confident, articulate and determined to improve conditions in Scotland. It has been obvious for years that Alex is highly intelligent, with a sharp wit and a mind that moves at an incredible speed, and that he has a deep knowledge of both economics and history. As First Minister he has displayed another quality, delicacy and diplomatic skill, in his dealings with other political leaders in Scotland and elsewhere. Iain MacWhirter in *The Herald* of 30th July 2007 described him as 'the first genuine political leader in Scottish democratic history'. Our progress to independence and the recovery of our role in international relations could not be in surer hands.

So we are now living in Scotland in a new age of optimism and hope. We felt it, to give one small example, when we discussed at the Edinburgh Branch of the party in July two resolutions which I had proposed for the National Conference in October, one on broadcasting and one on my proposal for a National Museum of Scottish Literature. Both were passed unanimously. We were all very conscious of the fact that such resolutions in the past had been little more than pious expressions of hope. Now they might actually produce results. We had, at last, a Scottish Government in office genuinely and enthusiastically committed to working for Scotland.

Independently of my resolution, action on broadcasting followed very soon afterwards. Early in August we were invited to a lecture about broadcasting which Alex Salmond was to give on the 8th in the round room of the Museum of Scotland. It was a crowded gathering of political commentators, broadcasters and people concerned about the problem which briefly is that Scotland, Scottish issues and programme makers are being increasingly disregarded as a consequence of control from London. 'Scotland,' Salmond said, 'as much as any other nation, needs to be a society dedicated to learning and communication.'

He announced the establishment of a Commission on Broadcasting to be chaired by Blair Jenkins, the former Head of News and Current Affairs of BBC Scotland who resigned in protest over the financial cuts imposed on it. The other members of the Commission who were announced a few days later, included prominent people from parties other than the SNP. This is another instance of Salmond's political dexterity. Immediate progress could not be made by the Scottish Parliament in which the SNP does not have an overall majority; but recommendations from such a Commission would be difficult to ignore. At the reception afterwards I heard nothing but praise for Salmond.

On the following Tuesday, such is the speed of action by this Government, Alex had a press conference at which he launched the White paper, *Choosing Scotland's Future: A National Conversation*. Next day he spoke about it at the Book Festival. This is a Government, not a party, document drafted by the Civil Service. The paper firmly asserts the basic point on which the whole depends:

> The people of Scotland remain sovereign and have the
> same right to choose the form of their own government as
> the peoples of other nations that have secured
> independence after periods of union with, or in, other
> states. (para 3.3)

It is lucid, comprehensive and balanced. It proposes a 'National Conversation' about the three possibilities: continuing the current constitutional arrangement with no or minimal change; extending the responsibilities devolved to Scotland; or taking the steps to allow Scotland to become a fully independent country. It contains the draft of a Bill for a referendum on independence.

All this was going on at the same time as the multifarious festivals which make Edinburgh a seething hotbed of thousands of performances of music, dance, theatre and comedy of all kinds from the supreme to the absurd. I am less involved than I used to be, especially as I am no longer reviewing, but I have taken part in two events. The first of these was in a debate, once again with Michael Fry and Christopher Whatley, about the origins of the Union of 1707. This time it was part of the Book Festival, which in its crowded programme of sixteen days brings together, as it says in its brochure, 'over 600 authors from over

35 different countries'. It is a great opportunity to meet people, a better chance to encounter and exchange ideas than even in a club or howf of eighteenth century Edinburgh.

My other small contribution was in a series of no fewer than 24 different 'conversations' about the history of the Festival which Richard Demarco had arranged to accompany an exhibition of part of his huge archive in the Scottish National Portrait Gallery. My conversation was with Roddy Martine and, of course, with the irrepressible Richard himself, on our recollections of the first Festival, sixty years ago. Riccy has done more than anyone to transform and invigorate Edinburgh.

Ian Scott, previous chairman of the Saltire Society, Cunni Rankin his successor and I had a meeting in early September with Fiona Hyslop, Cabinet Secretary for Education and Life-Long Learning, and with Linda Fabiani, Minister for Culture. They welcomed us warmly and we discussed for more than an hour broadcasting, education, the Scots language, and my proposal for a National Museum of Scottish Literature. On all of them we had a very positive response. Ian was right to remind us of the admirable report which the Scottish Consultative Council on the Curriculum drew up between 1996 and 1998 to deal with 'the problem of the inadequate attention given by Scottish schools to the languages, literature, history and culture of Scotland'. This was due for publication in 1998, but it was replaced by a short and emaciated summary because of the political pressure of the Labour Government.

This inadequacy of Scottish education is one of the basic problems which face Scotland. You cannot understand your own place in the world, and the situation in which you find yourself, if you have no knowledge of the past. This is not only a matter of culture, or intellectual understanding, but of basic self-confidence. As a consequence of the Union of 1707 there are many forces which tend to make Scots feel that they live in an unimportant backwater where everything is inferior to the great world outside. This destroys self-confidence and ambition and undermines effort and achievement. Broadcasting controlled by London is the most potent of these forces, but a population with little knowledge of the remarkable achievements and international influence of Scotland is particularly vulnerable. It is highly appropriate that Alex Salmond has taken the first step to deal with broadcasting by his establishment of the Commission. This is a problem which has concerned the Saltire Society for many years. The Society in fact began a new phase of its campaigning on the subject only last year.

I have been involved for years with both the SNP as Cultural Spokesman and with the Saltire Society in various capacities. Fundamentally, they share the same objective. It is well defined in the words of the Society's annual syllabus:

> The Saltire Society was founded in 1936 to encourage
> everything that might improve the quality of life in
> Scotland and restore the country to its proper place as a
> creative force in European civilisation. It seeks to preserve
> all that is best in Scottish tradition and to encourage new
> developments which can strengthen and enrich the
> country's cultural life.

There is a great deal for the SNP Government to do because so much is wrong with contemporary Scotland. Many of us are reasonably prosperous, well fed and well housed; but there is a substantial minority who live in poverty amid the plenty. In many international tables of comparison Scotland is well down among European countries in such matters as addiction to drugs or alcohol, premature death, violent crime. Many people still live in poverty, badly housed, ill-educated and deprived of hope. We are far below the level of achievement of the seventeenth and eighteenth centuries when, as Macaulay remarked, Scots were widely regarded as the most intelligent and accomplished people in Europe.

What has gone wrong? I suspect that the trouble began with the massive move, in the Lowlands as well as the Highlands, of population from the country to the towns in search of employment in the new industries. In the nineteenth century the Church of Scotland, which had concerned itself with social problems in the past, was preoccupied with the effects of the Disruption. That was a consequence of the imposition of patronage on the Church by the Westminster Parliament in violation of an Act associated with the Treaty of Union. Also in that century attention was focussed more on the Empire than on Scotland itself, and Scotland had no Government to concern itself with the miseries of the slums. The serious problem of social deprivation was neglected in the nineteenth century and we still suffer from the consequences.

A country like Scotland with its own traditions, geography, climate, economy, social habits and social problems needs it own government to respond to them. If you are governed by a larger neighbour, no matter how well disposed it may be, its major preoccupations are bound to be with its own concerns. You could even say that this is democratically proper since the views of the majority should prevail.

A government of our own with control of all aspects of policy and which can respond to our own needs is much more likely to find the right solutions than one in the south-east of England where conditions and attitudes are very different. This ability to respond rapidly to their own needs and opportunities is one of the reasons why the other small countries of Europe which have been liberated from external control have all become much more prosperous.

The advantages of small independent countries have been recognised for centuries. Two examples come from the Scottish Enlightenment of the eighteenth century. David Hume in his essay on *The Idea of a Perfect Commonwealth* wrote:

> A small commonwealth is the happiest government in the world within itself because everything lies under the eyes of the rulers.

Adam Fergusson in his *Essay on the History of Civil Society* (1767):

> We need not enlarge our communities in order to enjoy
> these advantages (by which he meant those of living in a
> civilised society). We frequently obtain them in the most
> remarkable degree where nations remain independent
> and are of a small extent.

Both of these essays were written more than fifty years after 1707 and were clearly a judgement on the effect of the Union.

In our concern for a prosperous economy we seem to have lost sight of another idea of the Scottish Enlightenment, that, in the words of Francis Hutcheson: 'The end of all civil power is acknowledged by all to be the safety and happiness of the whole body.'

Certainly a strong economy which enables the whole community to live comfortable and healthy lives is one of the requirements for this 'safety and happiness'; but it is not enough by itself. We need a peaceful and law-abiding society free from violence, and the abuse of alcohol and drugs; a well-educated society with a flourishing cultural and intellectual life and egalitarian in spirit. We are much more likely to achieve such a society if we recover control of our own affairs and are able to draw on the values of our own traditions.

We also need freedom from external threat. Paradoxically small independent countries are less likely to be exposed to this than larger ones with ambitions to act, even if it is beyond their present strength, as a world power. British governments have been guilty of this. Hence their addiction to nuclear weapons and their participation in the Iraq war with all the disasters which have followed. Independence would also give us the advantages of our own membership of the European Union and other international organisations with the right to express our own opinions and defend our own interests.

Another advantage of independence is that it will remove many of the grievances that trouble relations between Scotland and England. Many of these are a consequence of devolution. Many people in England, ignoring the proceeds of Scottish oil, seem to believe that Scotland is subsidised by the English taxpayer. They have a more legitimate grievance in objecting to Scottish members of the Westminster Parliament voting on such English policy matters as education and the health service, which in Scotland are the responsibility of the Scottish Parliament.

Scotland has many complaints. The reserving of innumerable subjects to the Westminster Parliament means that the Scottish Parliament cannot take the necessary action and Westminster is notoriously dilatory in finding time for Scottish business. It also means that economic policy is directed to English and not Scottish conditions and needs. Since cultural policy is devolved to Scotland, it is absurd that broadcasting, a major means of cultural expression, is reserved to Westminster. There are 17 pages in the list of such reserved matters.

On the other hand, with Scotland as an independent country with our own voice in Europe and as part of the European-wide market, we should be able to co-operate on most questions, but defend our own interests where we differ. We should be friendly and co-operative partners, not a disgruntled subordinate.

The success of the SNP in the election in May 2007 was already a sign that there had been a change in the mood of the people of Scotland. They were no longer prepared to tolerate an administration with little ambition for Scotland and mainly concerned to preserve the subordination to London. The first months of the energetic and skilful SNP Government rapidly enhanced the spirit of optimism and independence.

James Robertson remarked to me during the Book Festival that the speed of the change was astonishing. Perhaps the most remarkable proof of this was in the speech made by Wendy Alexander on 21st August 2007 when she accepted her 'coronation' as leader of the Scottish Labour Party. They had fought the Election by an insistence that the Devolution arrangement required no change. Only a day or two earlier Des Browne, the Secretary of State for Scotland in the Labour Cabinet in London, had repeated confidently that this was still the policy. But from parts of Alexander's speech one might suppose that she was a supporter of the SNP. Labour had lost the Election, she said, 'because the SNP were better able to capture the mood of the nation'. She was in favour of increased powers for the Scottish Parliament and wanted 'Scottish solutions for Scottish aspirations'.

The Scotland of poor performance, poor expectations and a poor opinion of itself seems already to be at an end. We used to set a good example to the rest of the world and we can do it again. ❑

6. The Way Ahead

Before I end this brief sequel, I should like to say a little, in this optimistic time, about my hopes and expectations for the immediate future.

Alex Salmond has predicted that Scotland will recover her independence by 2017. The competence of the SNP Government and its commitment to the interests of Scotland are now so obvious that it is highly probable that they will win a substantial majority in the election of 2011. They should then be able to call and win a referendum on independence. It is recognised both internationally and repeatedly by British Governments that a decision in favour of independence in such a referendum must be respected. There will then be a period of negotiation over the necessary arrangements with the British Government, the European Union and the United Nations. There should be no great difficulty or delay over this. The British Government handled such negotiations with their former colonies smoothly and rapidly, as I well remember because I was working in the Foreign Office at the time. Scotland is already part of the territory of the European Union and will remain so. As the recent example of Montenegro demonstrated, membership of the United Nations is likely to follow a successful referendum very quickly.

Some people argue that independence has little significance or value in our contemporary globalised world. That is absurd. Just because international organisations now have such an important role, it is vital for a country like Scotland to be recognised as an independent state because they alone have the right to be a member of these organisations and therefore able to express and defend their own interests and points of view.

There are many other reasons why we need independence and I mentioned some of them in my previous chapter. The fundamental reason was discussed recently in a book by Malcolm Anderson, *States and Nationalism in Europe since 1945,* in which he said:

> Nationalism is an expression of certain straightforward ideas which provide a framework for political life. . . Basic ideas are that most people belong to a national group which is reasonably homogeneous. These nations have characteristics – habits, ways of thinking and institutions – which clearly distinguish them from other national groups; that nations should be 'self-determining' and preferably have independent governments.

David McCrone in a review of the book (in Scottish *Affairs* No 38) concluded:

> Nationalism is not some aberrant philosophy responsible for the evils of the modern world. It is the keystone of liberal democracy.

I do not suppose that there can be any doubt that Scotland is pre-eminently such a national group with recognisable characteristics, which has survived despite all the pressures to conform to the ideas and tastes of the larger group with which it has been associated since 1603 and more closely since 1707. In the words of Neil Gunn, 'We have a history as old and distinctive as any country in Europe.'

In fact, Scotland was the first nation in post-classical Europe to express and defend these 'basic ideas'. The Declaration of Arbroath of 1320 is the first, and one of the most eloquent, expressions of it. We then defended our independence for 300 years against a larger and more powerful neighbour until in 1603 by a dynastic accident James VI became also King of England.

There are many obvious reasons why a distinctive country should govern itself in accordance with its ideas and aspirations. In recent years almost all the submerged nations in the empires and multi-national states have successfully asserted their independence. As I mentioned in chapter 4, I have been fortunate enough to visit some of these newly independent nations fairly frequently during the last ten years or so, especially Estonia and Slovenia. This has been an inspiring experience. Their rapid increase in prosperity has been very obvious, but so has the visible increase in the contentment and optimism of the people, a clear demonstration of the pursuit of happiness. In both of these small countries the people seem to me to be very like the Scots in many ways, fond of their country, instinctively friendly and free of arrogance and pretension. Their experience is a convincing demonstration of the advantages of independence.

Why has Scotland fallen so far behind in this wide movement of international liberation? It is true, of course, that the British state has a formidable propaganda machine at its disposal, especially since the creation of the BBC. Long before that it exerted itself to persuade the Scots that the Union was beneficial to them, as it was in many ways in the nineteenth and early twentieth centuries when the Empire still existed. Some people still seem to believe that they are likely to be safer and more prosperous as part of a larger state than on their own in a smaller one. On the contrary, the larger state, especially if it has ambitions to cling to the status of a major power, is much more likely to become involved in international conflict and become a target for retaliation. British involvement in the Iraq War and its consequences is an example.

Nor is an economic advantage for a smaller state to be subordinated to a larger. The larger partner inevitably gives preference to is own interests. When England started to press for the Union, Andrew Fletcher predicted that one of its effects would be to draw wealth to the south-east corner of England. That is precisely what has happened and increasingly in recent years, with the steady erosion of control of Scottish companies to the south and the seizure of the assets of oil in Scottish waters by the British Government.

The advantages of independence are not only economic; the psychological are probably even more important. As Eric Linklater said in his book, *The Lion and the Unicorn:*

> I believe people degenerate when they lose control of
> their own affairs, and, as a corollary, that resumption of
> control may induce regeneration. To any nation the
> essential vitamin is responsibility.

To this degeneration has been added, through our education, an almost complete ignorance of our history and our contribution to the world, with an inevitable undermining of self-respect and self-confidence.

Some people apparently tell the pollsters that they are opposed to independence. They may simply be afraid of any change or strongly imbued with the idea of Britishness. I suspect that the most common reason is simply that they have not thought about the question at all, nor perhaps about any other political issue. This general indifference to matters of importance, which the ancient Greeks would have regarded as idiocy, is unfortunately not uncommon.

The British Government has several reasons for a desire to hold on to Scotland. Scottish oil is an important source of revenue. The Clyde is a useful base for nuclear submarines, even if most Scots disapprove of them. Scotland is a source of recruits for British forces. Scottish members of the Westminster Parliament have a strong personal reason for clinging to the Union. They depend on it for their comfortable and well-paid jobs.

In recent years there has been a sharp increase in the number of people who fail to vote in elections. They apparently take no interest in public affairs. According to press reports, many of them say that they think that all politicians are the same and that votes make no difference. The absurdity of that idea has been exposed by the immediate transformation of Scotland by the election of an SNP Government. I think that this failure to take a serious interest in politics is a symptom of the widespread retreat from thought and an intelligent approach to life which has become apparent since about the late 1950s.

This change has been very apparent in the programmes of the BBC. It is discussed in David Robb's recent biography of Alexander Scott, the poet who died in 1989. For years his plays had been eagerly accepted by the BBC; but suddenly in the 1950s they began to refuse them. Robb attributes this to 'the great cultural shift from a national culture dominated by middle-class taste to one driven by a new working-class bias'. This may be one way of expressing it, but I think that the change was probably due to the influence of modern marketing methods. This is the doctrine that you should address the largest possible market whose tastes are detected by surveys of opinion. It means deliberately seeking to please the largest common denominator of the population, not a different class, but a different level of intelligence. At its origin the BBC sought to educate as well as entertain; it now seeks the least demanding form of entertainment.

Because of the scarcity of intelligent comment on serious issues and very little Scottish content of all kinds on the BBC and broadcasting generally, this is an important issue for Scotland.

Scotland has been celebrated in the past for its aspirations towards an egalitarian society and its high standards of education for all. In recent years we have fallen behind many countries in both respects.

It used to be widely accepted that a society could not be contented and successful unless the available wealth was distributed fairly evenly to all its members since a wide divergence between the rich and the poor was likely to stimulate greed, envy, social tension and crime. For example, Aldous Huxley in his book, *Ends and Means*, which he wrote in the 1940s, said:

> To obtain complete equality of income for all is probably impossible and perhaps even undesirable. But certain steps in the direction of equalisation can and undoubtedly ought to be taken. Even in capitalist countries the principle not only of the minimum but also of the maximum wage has already been admitted. Within the last twenty years it has generally been agreed that there are limits beyond which incomes and personal accumulations of capital ought not to go.

Under Blair the British Government has legislated for a minimum wage but has abandoned any attempt to limit the maximum. Wages in some occupations, and not always the most socially useful, have soared to absurdly high levels. Six million pounds a year to the manager of the England football team, for instance. Nobody needs this level of income. What can they possibly do with it? It stimulates envy and discontent which encourages frantic consumerism and the accumulation of debt. Surplus wealth could be used to help the poor and disadvantaged. I think that most of us in Scotland would prefer to live in a fair society without extremes of wealth and poverty.

Education is of vital importance because the happiness, good sense and prosperity of the country depend on it. I have already mentioned the extraordinary neglect by our schools of Scottish history, literature and culture generally as well as the Scots language. It looks very much like a systematic attempt to indoctrinate us with the sort of Britishness which is in fact Englishness. England is a country with many excellent qualities and proud achievements, but so is Scotland. We cannot understand our present without some knowledge of our past and ignorance of our own achievements destroys self-confidence.

Scottish history is therefore an essential part of Scottish education and the SNP Scottish Government have already taken the first steps to give it its proper place in the curriculum of the schools. It is a history which involves much of the rest of the world because Scotland played an important part in many other European countries before the Union and in the former British Empire afterwards. World history is too vast a subject to be taught in any detail in the schools, but they should aim at a general sense of the main outlines.

Scottish literature is another valuable subject, not only because it is one of the great literatures of Europe, but because it is a record of our experiences, emotions and ideas. The Scots language should be studied as the vehicle of much of the best of this literature. It has a rich vocabulary which is often the best expression of what we want to say and it encourages bilingualism and the acquisition of other languages. Scottish arts, music and dance should also be studied as an essential and delightful part of our national life.

The independent Scotland to which we look forward should be ambitious. Many people have suggested that we should aim at a new Scottish Enlightenment, offering new and liberating ideas to the world as we did in the eighteenth century. When I gave my Rectorial Address as Rector of Dundee University in April 1989, I quoted two men who had predicted such a future. Compton Mackenzie gave his Rectorial Address in 1931 in Glasgow when he like me had been a successful SNP candidate in a Rectorial Election. Although the immediate outlook was then very much less encouraging than it is now, he said that he did not believe that Scotland was dying, but was 'about to live with a fullness of life undreamed of yet.' I think that we are now very much closer to that fullness of life.

My other quotation was from Peter Jones, the Professor of Philosophy at Edinburgh University, who had published an essay in the *Glasgow Herald* about a month before in which he said:

'Scotland must proclaim itself as unashamedly intellectual,

the thinking nation, recognising no position as final, all claims as provisional, defiantly open to new avenues, steadfastly sceptical of current understanding, resolutely resistant to the narrowing categories of established boundaries of investigation.'

Why do so many people have such an ambition for Scotland? I suppose it is mainly because they see no reason why Scotland which has given so many new ideas to the world in the past should not do so again They believe that we have the capacity, when we are free to make our own decisions, to reject many of the absurdities of contemporary life and to suggest a more rational way to create a richer, happier and more intelligent society.   ❏

Index

Other books from Argyll Publishing

www.argyllpublishing.com